Coaching
For Missional Leadership

Coaching
For Missional Leadership

Growing and Supporting Pioneers in
Church Planting and Fresh Expressions

BOB HOPKINS &
FREDDY HEDLEY

ACPI BOOKS
www.acpi.org.uk

ACPI Books
Philadelphia Campus
6 Gilpin Street
Sheffield
S6 3BL

T: 0114 278 9378
F: 0114 278 9600
admin@acpi.org.uk

ISBN 978-0-95593-6-319

Published 2008 by ACPI Books in partnership with Fresh Expressions
www.freshexpressions.org.uk

Unless otherwise indicated, biblical quotations are taken from the New
International Version (NIV) © 1973, 1978, 1984 by the International
Bible Society.

Cover photograph by Kath Atkins. Design by MPH.

CONTENTS

FOREWORD

We learn in many ways, both formal and informal, but, as I look at the relationship between Jesus and his disciples I am struck by the way he taught them and the differences from much of our curriculum-led teaching. Jesus offered each of his disciples personal learning based on an understanding of their abilities and needs in a way that is only possible in a mentoring or coaching relationship.

Fresh Expressions uses the term 'companion' for a range of people who accompany others on their explorations of Christian mission. A companion is someone with whom, literally, you share bread (latin *com-panis*). The eating of a meal together is one of the most intimate of human activities and sets the tone for relationships in which we can share our lives. It is no accident that Jesus set his most challenging teaching to his disciples in the context of a meal.

There are many types of Christian mission companions. Among them are spiritual directors and church consultants of various kinds. Fresh Expressions has found from experience that what are variously called *coaches* and *mentors* are extremely beneficial for those developing fresh expressions of church. We advise all who want to tread this path to look for a coach or mentor and also advise churches and denominations to look for people who seek such a companion for their fresh expressions projects. We believe that looking for such a companion is a sign of a person with a spirit open to learning and the leading of the Holy Spirit.

Over the years of his ministry Bob Hopkins and his wife Mary have coached and mentored many involved in church planting and now what is termed fresh expressions. Working with

Freddy, Bob has condensed his years of experience into this guide. Together they have written what, I believe, will become one of the standard text books on the subject.

I hope you enjoy reading this as much as I have and that your reading of it will enrich your walk with God.

Pete Pillinger
Fresh Expressions core team member
and Methodist Connexional Fresh Expressions Missioner

Pete is also the co-ordinator of coaching and mentoring for Fresh Expressions.

INTRODUCTION

With the publication in 2004 of the Anglican report *Mission Shaped Church*, there has been an acceleration in the growing movement of mission emerging right across the church. Fresh expressions of church have been planned, birthed and developed to a point where they now form a significant mark on the radar – not just of the church, but of society as a whole. New bridges are being forged, new people reached, new communities formed.

To help support, encourage and resource this movement new patterns of ministry are being recognised and a number of new forms of training have emerged to see people equipped and released to lead these fresh expressions. These include the new Ordained and Lay Pioneer Minister guidelines as well as the *mission shaped intro* and *mission shaped ministry* courses from Fresh Expressions. This has led to an increasing number of leaders in the church, mostly lay leaders, who are filled with vision, excitement, commitment and most importantly, a sense of God's call and vocation.

The training initiatives that are required need to be based on a process of design and understanding. As well as providing sound missional and theological principles and practical skills, the training needs to be delivered in a way, and over a period, that supports practitioners on their journey of planning and initiating new mission initiatives or fresh expressions. In such a philosophy of training for pioneer teams, coaching and mentoring needs to be integral to the process and ideally learning networks will emerge along the way.

In response to these needs, both to support and further equip pioneer leaders and teams, a number of approaches have already been adopted. These include consulting, direct training, mentoring, coaching and accompaniment. All are important and carry enormous potential value, but in this book we want to concentrate particularly on mentoring and coaching as being essential for every missional leader's life and ministry.

In these few pages we will explain some of the background to coaching and mentoring, as well as exploring the processes and skills involved and how it can make a real difference to a leader's approach to their ministry and the resulting fruit. However, primarily this book seeks to be a tool that those involved in coaching and mentoring relationships can use.

It may be that missional leaders being coached/mentored will find this helpful to further understand the priorities and processes involved. It may even be a useful spark of ideas for how a leader can in turn coach the other key leaders in their fresh expression. Mainly, though, this is a tool for the coaches and mentors themselves.

> *Throughout this book we will be looking at issues that relate both to coaching and mentoring, and can be applied to either depending on which process you are using. However, though we want to make it clear here that all the material in this book is written for both, from this point on we are only going to be using the term coaching. This is purely for simplicity of communication, and not because we are implying that one process is better than the other.*

The material here is largely based on the *Missional Church Coaching* course developed by Bob & Mary Hopkins, but we must also acknowledge the influence and input of others. In particular, we would point towards Bob Logan, from *Coachnet*[1] and the *CRM basic coaching course*[2]; John Whitmore, and his book *Coaching for Performance: Growing People, Performance and Purpose*[3]; Steve Nicholson and the *Vineyard Church Planting Coaches Manual*; St Thomas' Church in Sheffield (as well as The Order of Mission and 3 Dimensional Ministries), where the LifeShapes principles have been developed[4]; and Richard Priestley from Church Army, who has inputted directly on some of the material here and helped with some of the recent developments of our *Missional Church Coaching* course.

Many who have been identified as potential coaches of missional leaders will have been on the CRM basic coaching course mentioned above, in order to acquire the habits of listening and asking good questions. This book is written to be an ongoing resource that naturally follows and builds on this excellent training.

WHO WILL DO THE COACHING/MENTORING?

But before we get into exploring the principles we should ask, 'Who will do the coaching?' As we answer this question we quickly recognise that those coming forward to meet the need will already bring different experience and skills in the two key fields of coaching and of mission. These differences will directly affect the priorities for their training and equipping. Clearly these will be determined by the need to fill in the gaps where skills and experience are weak or absent, or merely to complement and refresh stronger areas. The matrix overleaf (originally produced by Pete Pillinger) helpfully highlights the

---

[1] See www.coachnet.org

[2] Run by Ian Hamilton in the UK - www.crmnet.org.uk

[3] 3rd edition published by Nicholas Brealy Publishing Ltd, 2002

[4] The LifeShapes principles have been written up in *The Passionate Church* and *A Passionate Life*, both published by Nexgen, 2004 & 2005 respectively.

possible range of strengths of experience, against weaker areas to be addressed.

This book majors on the bottom two squares of the matrix

It is important to recognise that this book deals with the generic principles of coaching and mentoring and applies them to missional leaders and pioneers. Hence these chapters particularly address the needs of those represented by the two squares at the bottom of the diagram with low knowledge and experience in these areas. However, they should also support, refresh and extend those in the top two squares.

Ideally those coaching missional pioneers and fresh expressions planters, should have first had experience of both these ministries and be familiar with training for pioneers such as *mission shaped ministry*. They should also be regularly updating themselves with the latest good practice in pioneering mission. And one of the best ways is to be a regular visitor and fully conversant with the content of the Fresh Expressions knowledge bank, *Share*, which can be accessed at www.sharetheguide.org. The appendix to this book provides a brief outline of some of the key areas to be familiar with in pioneering mission.

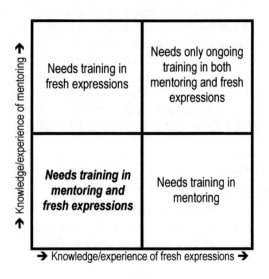

↑ Knowledge/experience of mentoring ↑

Needs training in fresh expressions	Needs only ongoing training in both mentoring and fresh expressions
Needs training in mentoring and fresh expressions	Needs training in mentoring

➔ Knowledge/experience of fresh expressions ➔

12

1

BASIC PRINCIPLES

As we mentioned in the introduction there are a number of processes used across the church to enable leader development and project support. Amongst these there are three that consistently stand out above the rest: *consulting*, *mentoring* and *coaching*. These terms are often used interchangeably and a fourth term, accompaniment, is also used by many, either to describe the most non-directive approach or as a general term that can cover all three! However, we think that there are important differences between the processes and, although all may not accept our definitions, we prefer to use the terms in the following way[5]:

TASK-CENTRED CONSULTANCY

Consultancy is a process that concentrates primarily on a task. Be that a mission initiative, planting a fresh expression or implementing changes across the church,

---

[5] The Foundation for Church Leadership have produced an excellent on-line resource paper, *Using or Being a Consultant, Mentor or Coach*. In it they encourage all churches to invest in such outside support and give helpful definitions of consultant, mentor and coach, which are not dissimilar from ours here. This can be found on their website at www.churchleadershipfoundation.org

a consultant's job is to enter into that situation from outside and bring their expertise and wider perspective for the purpose of helping to bring the task to fruition.

PERSON-CENTRED MENTORING

Mentoring is a term used by different people to describe a variety of methods and aims, some of which overlap with spiritual direction. But we see it most helpfully referring to what is usually a long-term a process that concentrates primarily on the development of a person. This would therefore be focused on their personal walk with Jesus, the growth of their faith and how they live it, as well as how they develop as a leader. In this view, a mentor is there to encourage and affirm; to challenge and hold accountable; for the development of the soul, character, gifts and skills of the mentee. Mentoring usually has a high value on non-directive processes involving reflective learning for greatest ownership by the mentee.

CALLING-CENTRED COACHING

Coaching (also sometimes used interchangeably with mentoring) we prefer to see as a process that applies when both task and person are involved. Put together, these two elements collectively give a sense of calling, where the task and the person set aside to carry it out, are intertwined and it is impossible to listen to God about the one without also hearing about the other. A common example of this would be any level of leadership. The leader and what they are leading are inseparable from one another as God always uses one to enforce and grow the other.

14

Given that mentoring, as we are using the term, is more specifically for the growth of a person regardless of task, when thinking about developing missional projects or fresh expressions we are generally left with two considerations: i) bring in consultants to offer their expertise and perspective; or ii) invite in a coach to take the leader through a process of development that will be worked out through the exercise of their ministry. Both are important and not exclusive of one another in any way. In fact, they can work well together.

To see where the differences in the two approaches come, consider the world of sport for a moment. In any given sport there are a number of people that surround the athletes and team players, but the two that we are most familiar with in terms of inputting on a sports person's performance are their coach, who takes them through a process of development on a one to one level, and the sports pundits, who comment and advise out of their own expertise and independent perspective.

Clearly an athlete will gain very different benefits from each. From the pundit – in some ways the equivalent of a consultant (though as a rule an uninvited one!) - they will get a level of immediate honesty that won't take into consideration any emotional response. This can be very healthy and offers much needed reality checks. A pundit also draws from experience and extra knowledge gained from watching how one athlete stands up against another, and the trends over time. Furthermore, a pundit has an external, detached view and works in response to situations observed.

A coach on the other hand is on the inside and isn't limited to response, but can also direct. They can help the athlete not only to learn from their past successes and mistakes, but also to be driven by their goals and potential. The sports coach knows only too well the importance not only of technique, talent and skills but also personality, attitude and confidence. To further build on this the coach develops an intimate knowledge of the athlete – what will motivate them, their aspirations, their priorities and so on. They are able to take the athlete through a process based on an understanding of what will challenge without hurting, what will motivate without daunting, what will stretch without breaking.

The coach sees the daily ups and downs, how the athlete responds from determination or frustration, and then is able to tailor their coaching to turn this to the athlete's advantage. And not only do they do this, but they hold them accountable for their progress, making the relationship between coach and athlete paramount – each is dependent on the progress of the other.

Taking this back to the world of missional church and fresh expressions, we might draw the following differences between coaching and consultancy, as seen in the table below.

Coaching		Consultancy
Ongoing	v	Fixed series of sessions
Process	v	Problem / issue focused
Person & task	&	Process / task focused
Relationship	&	Information based
Action & review	v	Detached & theoretical
Accountability	v	Little or none

WHERE IS YOUR MAIN FOCUS?

With these differences in approach there are also different aspects that form the main focus. In seeking to come alongside to help in missional church contexts there are two potential main objectives. The first is to help to make the missional church enterprise as effective as possible. As we have already explored, this would fall more in the territory of the consultant.

The second is to help the person become the most effective missional church leader possible, thereby increasing the effectiveness and fruit of the fresh expression or mission initiative as a consequence. This should always be a significant focus of the coach. Whilst always keeping the **task** in mind, the **person** is often the starting point and the measure.

Obviously one needs to have both goals in mind and we are certainly not setting one against the other. But being conscious of your emphasis as a coach will make a tremendous difference to your style and approach... as well as to the outcome. Here is a scale that can be used to help coaches to address where their main focus is:

The Project v Person Scale

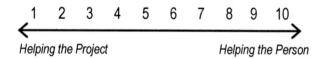

As you begin to coach your missional leaders, have this scale in mind and after a session check yourself against it in terms of where your focus tends to be, and where you would like it to be. There is a review sheet in Appendix II to help you do this.

Repeat this task as the coaching relationship develops to see whether you are getting closer or veering further away from your desired score and focus. As a general guide, a coach wants to keep their score above five.

At this point it may also be helpful to consider the focus of the coachee, as it is both different from the coach but crucially also informs so much of whether the person or the task is being engaged in the coaching at any one time. Here, we could draw a scale between 'Awareness' and 'Responsibility'. On the one side there is the need for the missional leader to engage in self-assessment and clarification of their context, and on the other is the need for the coachee to explore and understand what they need to do to move forwards. The coaching process will always be swinging between these two, depending on where the coachee needs to be focusing.

WHAT GIVES A COACH AUTHORITY?

It can be important at the start of the coaching process to understand where the coach's authority is drawn from, as this too will influence how the coaching relationship develops and what form it takes. CRM have helpfully identified four sources of a coach's authority. It is quite possible for a missional leader to identify more than one, even all four of these in the coach they invite, but it is likely that one will be the primary reason for a coach being chosen. The four possible sources are:

Positional authority: The coach is appointed based on the role they perform in relation to the missional leader. They may be the person with some direct 'line manager' type of authority over them, or such a 'line manager' may have brought them in. The danger here is that the coach could instruct or limit the missional leader according to his or her own agenda. It can also stifle the depth of accountability if missional pioneers feel they can't explore things they don't think they do well. On the other hand, the relationship is likely to be less occasional and more naturally a shared journey. The more that institutional authority plays a part in a coaching relationship, the harder the coach will have to work to avoid this altering the coaching dynamic. The process can still be extremely fruitful but it is unlikely to deliver all that a good independent coach could bring

Expertise-based authority: In this case the coach is invited, based on the missional leader identifying them as having the key experience and expertise that can unlock their potential. This carries with it the benefit that the coach is immediately perceived as helpful, and the coachee will be very open to working through any question they are asked. There is, however, a danger of the coachee too easily tending to ask, 'What should I do?' and wanting to be spoon-fed.

Spiritual authority: Here the coach is recognised for their maturity, wisdom and discernment. Where in 'positional authority' the authority is given partly by structure and circumstance, and in 'expertise-based authority' it is given partly from acquired experience, in this case the authority relates more to character and God-given qualities and spiritual gifts that have been identified (although God is also involved in the other forms of authority). This form of authority has the potential for speaking powerfully into difficult situations. But care is needed to avoid any potential for spiritual pride or spiritual over-emphasis. This can also lead to excessive influence and the 'What should I do?' question again needs to be guarded against.

Relational authority: In this last case, the coaching relationship is based on an existing valued relationship. And it is likely that at least one of the previous three authority sources have contributed to the missional leader identifying their chosen coach. This authority is given by the pioneer based on existing trust, but this must also be confirmed in the practicalities of the new coaching process. The strength of this relationship lies in the certainty of the coachee that the coach believes in them, but it must be recognised that this is still an authority that develops over time, so being able to discern how well the level of trust is growing is vital for the coach not to overreach themselves too early.

SO WHAT ARE THE BASICS?

When calling is the main issue, coaching is the process that can best help both the missional leader and the initiative they lead. Throughout the rest of this book we will come to be familiar with the different layers involved in this dynamic process of coaching. To get us started, though, let's consider some of the main points we have made so far in closer detail...

1. Coaching is a Relationship

From the outset the coach needs to recognise that their relationship with the coachee is an entity in itself. For coaching to be effective it relies on the strength of this relationship between the coach and the missional leader. Although there is a focus on task, as mentioned before, it is always in the context of the person and it is essential that the needs and 'speed of progress' of the person are a high priority of discernment for the coach.

It is also important to recognize that in entering into a coaching relationship, the coach becomes a part of the story of the fresh expression involved. The effectiveness of the coach impacts the effectiveness of the missional leader, which in turn impacts the effectiveness of the fresh expression. This means that the relationship between coach and leader needs to be very strong - with a high degree of trust in the coach's discernment and wisdom from the leader, and a high degree of belief in the leader's vision and heart from the coach.

2. Coaching is a Process

Coaching is an intentional process. The key dynamic of the relationship between coach and missional leader is that it is a shared journey. There needs to be an understanding that as in all journeys, the destination is not the be all and end all – the process of getting there is just as important.

There are different ways of expressing this process, but the one we have used often with the greatest success is the Discipleship Square, which was developed as a part of LifeShapes by Mike Breen[6]. The diagram on page 21 illustrates the process that we all go through when we are called to a new and challenging role such as missional church leadership. There are typically four stages we go through and the help or leadership we need changes as we progress round the square from D1 (discipleship stage 1) to D4 (discipleship stage 4).

---

[6] For more details on LifeShapes, including Mike Breen's own teaching on the square as well as the other seven shapes, they are published in *The Passionate Church* and *A Passionate Life*, both written by Mike Breen and Walk Kallestad and published by Nexgen (2004 and 2005 respectively).

As you will see, the first stage is one of high enthusiasm, keenness to explore new territory, filled with hopes and excitement for what might happen. Typically this might be expressed by *high enthusiasm, low competence*. At this stage it doesn't matter if people don't know what they are doing – enthusiasm will drive them and it is enough that the leader knows what they are doing (or so people might assume!). In response to this a classical or directive style of leadership is needed. Vision must be communicated well and often, and the leader can adopt a 'come follow me' message.

The second stage comes when time and experience of the journey has eroded the enthusiasm to leave the cold hard facts of the situation. A person or team may still be low on competence, but now they know it! So the result is *low enthusiasm and low competence*. In response to this stage the leader needs to adopt a more personal approach, drawing closer alongside the people/team, encouraging them to stay focused on the vision, drawing faith from the call and helping them to see where God is growing them. It is during this second stage (or D2) that the coaching style is what best helps a leader or team to progress.

The temptation is so often to give up or re-negotiate the vision whilst in D2. It seems too hard and can feel like it was a bad idea all along. However, it is an essential part of the growing process and you need to go through this if the next stage is to be reached.

The corner begins to be turned when experience builds into the development of both skills and understanding. This D3 stage can be expressed as *growing enthusiasm, growing competence* – leading to the team beginning to see the first fruits of their labour and wanting to be more actively involved as they begin to believe again that they are on the right track. The best leadership style to adopt here is to be more consultative and consensus driven – working very much as a team of equals and involving the whole team in each part of the leadership process.

Finally, entering stage D4 the skills and experience become such that the team are able to step into being the leaders themselves. They have reached *high enthusiasm, high competence* and the time has come to hand the work over to them fully. This releases the leader to look for the next phase of their calling and it successfully multiplies what God is doing, so that now there is the potential for two or more teams where there was only one. The leadership style for D4 is one of delegating and releasing.

The Discipleship/Leadership Style Square

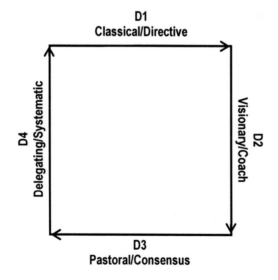

For a coach coming alongside a pioneer team leader an understanding of this four-stage process should help in two ways. First, as an 'outside' coach with this process in mind, you can observe and be sensitively appropriate to the person's progress from initial high enthusiasm but low experience and high confidence but low competence, through to very low confidence, before confidence and competence build into D3 and D4. Recognising these stages of your coachee's journey will help you interpret the dynamics to them.

Secondly, whilst accompaniment is helpful throughout this process, there is a sense in which the relationship of coach to coachee and the style of support will vary over time to mirror the styles of each phase for the pioneer leader. Whilst the coach may never fully adopt the directive style appropriate to a leader in D1, he/she should be sensitive to this progression and adjust his/her approach accordingly, moving to a lighter and lighter touch as the leader grows in confidence and competence through the process/project. Learning to discern where the leader is up to in this progression is a key skill for the coach to acquire.

3. Coaching relies on Feedback

The coaching relationship relies on space being given for the missional leader to reflect on the conclusions and action from previous coaching sessions and to give honest feedback. There also needs to be permission given for the coach to give honest feedback of their observations and perspective on how the calling and project are progressing.

4. Coaching values Accountability

Right at the heart of this coaching relationship and process is a high value of accountability. Coaching is not meant to be a series of disconnected observations or problem-solving. Issues will be revisited, challenges followed up and victories built on.

Honesty and vulnerability are crucial for the shared journey to genuinely reflect what God is doing and saying, and for the coach and missional leader to best be sensitive to God's leading, encouraging and challenging. This takes us back to the central importance of the relationship... there needs to be a strong sense of commitment and trust to be able to sustain this level of honesty.

A DEFINITION

Putting these four aspects together, Bob Logan and others have come up with the following definition:

> Coaching is intentionally helping someone else perform to their highest potential. It is a helping role to unlock someone's potential in pursuit of their goals. It is helping people be successful... where success is knowing God's will for your life and putting it into practice[7].

Coaching is fluid and dynamic. It has the potential to be both structured and yet spontaneous. There is both a recognized procedure for discussion, listening, giving new insight and even action; and also room for the Holy Spirit to break in and change the direction. It is both practical and heart-centred, fuelled by encouragement and challenge.

---

[7] Bob Logan & Sherilyn Carlton, *Coaching 101*, Churchsmart, 2003, p.23.

25

BUT KEEP IN MIND...

Yes this is a process that can be applied to anyone in the sense that there is a level of procedure to be followed. However, as we have identified, at the very heart of it this is a relational process. Consequently, we can see that it may not be right to coach anyone or everyone. For the relational strength to shine through, there are a few necessary requirements between the coach and the missional church leader. As you are considering who to coach, ask yourself these questions:

1. Is there some 'chemistry' between us?

The coaching relationship relies on fruitful two-way dialogue, flexibility from both sides to learn new wisdom and a desire to go on that journey together. It is not just a mechanical system that requires a set number of skills. For the coaching relationship to work there needs to be some chemistry. This is more than respect or trust – conversation and discussion need to come naturally; the people concerned need to understand one another and form a reliance on one another; and there needs to be a mutual sense of excitement about what can be learnt.

2. Do I believe in him/her?

The coach must have conviction in what they are doing, and at the heart of this must be the conviction that the leader they are coaching is worth the investment. Coaching is going to involve a lot of time, energy, care and attention, and it is all poured into this one relationship. So you need to be sure that you can really see the potential in the leader and their vision, and that you genuinely want them to succeed and want to be a privileged part of their development.

3. Do I have faith in what they want to do?

In the same way as believing in them personally, you need also to believe in what they want to achieve – be that a church plant, fresh expression or mission initiative. It isn't enough to only invest in the leader. As we have already seen, coaching is built on a *relationship* with a *purpose*... it must have both to succeed. It is therefore vital that the coach shares a belief and passion for both the general and specific purpose they will be addressing. Also, coaching inevitably involves lots of investment in the leader's ministry and the other people involved. Therefore it is important to have a sense that the aims and objectives are something you would want to see grow and flourish.

THE THREE FOCUSES OF MISSIONAL CHURCH COACHING

Having established these basics, we can summarize by breaking them down into the following three focuses that coaches need to have in their mind through the process:

The Leader(s): This includes their character, relationships, spiritual development, skills, experience and personal study.

The Project (and team): This includes the vision, any processes and strategy, its growth and fruit, and the ongoing developing relationship between the leader and the rest of the team.

The Coaching Relationship: This distinct entity itself involves modelling multiplication and a culture of release. This means that coaching should also produce a by-product of passing on effective leadership as well as being a leadership style in itself.

As we emphasised earlier, it is really helpful to see the coach-pioneer relationship as an entity in its own right with a life of its own, apart from the pioneer and the project. In this way we can visualize the three elements involved in coaching pioneers as represented in the triangle below and the coach can then regularly review the balanced development of the three elements.

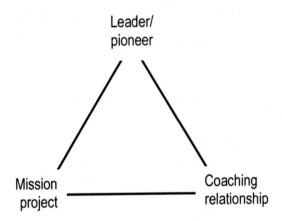

Leader/
pioneer

Mission
project

Coaching
relationship

AIMS OF COACHING SESSIONS AND VISITS

These three focuses, represented in the triangle, will form the themes of each coaching session/visit, as we will see in more detail when we come to look at the practical processes of coaching in later chapters. But what about the overall aims of these sessions/visits? Here are a few suggestions for what the coach will be looking to achieve:

- A broader/fuller perspective (God's view!)
- Observing the leader and the project
- Pinpointing crucial issues and blockages to success
- Referencing the appropriate core missional principles as they relate to project and stage
- Helping them generate creative and original ideas
- Building a functional relationship to develop the leader
- Encouraging and raising faith
- Identifying and understanding key skills
- Clarifying issues and getting focus
- Confronting errors and solving problems together
- Reaching decisions, both for personal development and study, as well as project implementation
- Praying and listening to God
- Setting an agreed program of action and study for future review

WHY COACH MISSIONAL LEADERS?

Now that we have looked at the basics of what coaching is, let us conclude by considering why it is so important. Missional church leadership and 'leadership for change' is a highly demanding, complex and practical enterprise and those of us involved need all the help we can get. More than that, we need to receive the help in a form that enables us to learn as effectively as possible through the process, as well as to implement the 'change process' or 'project' as successfully as possible. Coaching is one of the best ways to learn whilst being helped to lead missional church and here are four common reasons why:

1. Need to know

It can be tempting right from the start of a project for missional leaders to search for all the information they can to inform every possible step they might have to take. But doing so invariably leaves people overloaded and not well placed to access what they need when they need it. The most effective help in a long and complex process is to discover mainly the principles that shape the application of the next phase. Coaching accompanies the progress of the project and addresses only the immediate presenting issues enabling them to have full attention.

2. Experience ahead of input

Like *need to know*, it's clear that the motivation to learn (and consequently the best retention and integration of principles) is when you are 'hungry' to gain the knowledge. And this is usually because you are stretched by the immediate practical challenge of new experiences. The coach can draw alongside the leader at intervals during the development of the missional church process precisely when this motivational impetus is at work, so that insights and reflections have maximum chance of effecting action and change.

3. Show and tell

If we are to get the most effective help for implementation, and at the same time to learn and grow, then **demonstration** as well as **information** is powerful. Good coaching illustrates in the immediate practical context and mission challenge, how principles work.

Academic training tends to follow the order *orientate, equip, (only then) involve.*

Whereas the process of supporting, developing and training practitioners through coaching, follows the order *orientate, involve, equip (as you go).*

4. Non-formal learning

Coaching forms part of what can collectively be called non-formal learning processes. These are exactly the most appropriate forms of learning for a practical undertaking and particularly for one that requires exploration of something new rather than copying what already exists. Apprenticeship is the most characteristic non-formal learning process and coaching has similar characteristics. The diagram below depicts how non-formal learning works alongside the two other learning processes of formal and socialisation learning. We will return to this and look further into these areas of learning in chapter four, on *Processes of Learning.* But for now we see that coaching is non-formal learning that involves intentional processes, earthed in practicalities and opening up non-traditional outcomes.

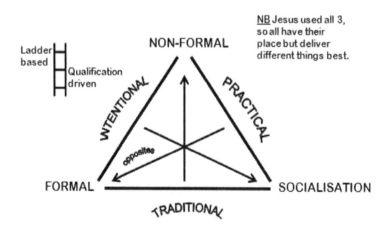

NB Jesus used all 3, so all have their place but deliver different things best.

31

YOUR NOTES ON THE CHAPTER...

2

THE BIBLICAL BASIS

Coaching is a thoroughly biblical process. Throughout the Old and New Testaments there are repeated examples of key relationships where one person draws alongside another to help them achieve their potential: Jethro advising Moses, Elisha learning from Elijah, Jesus teaching his disciples, Barnabas encouraging first Saul and then Mark. Read through carefully and there are more examples to find.

Often these relationships have more than one dynamic to them. Jesus was more than a coach to the disciples. He was their friend, their leader, their tutor, their example, and their saviour. Yet he was still their coach. Similar can be said of the other examples.

In order to further establish the relevance of coaching from a biblical point of view we will look more closely at four particular passages. These are all from the New Testament and give us an idea both of how Jesus models some of our key coaching values and processes, as well as how this was then continued into the early church.

Before we begin with our first exploration, into the account of the sending of the seventy-two, let's just consider again the definition of coaching proposed in chapter one:

Coaching is intentionally helping someone else perform to his or her highest potential. It is a helping role to unlock someone's potential in pursuit of their goals. It is helping people be successful... where success is knowing God's will for your life and putting it into practice.

Keep this in mind as we look at how leaders were raised, released and reviewed in their ongoing ministry. How did Jesus draw the best out of those he coached? How did Barnabas? How did Paul?

THE SENDING OF THE 72

We read about Jesus sending out the seventy-two in Luke 10:1-24. Already Jesus has sent out the twelve in chapter nine and gathered them back together for retreat and reflection. He has also since fed the 5,000, explored with the twelve the question of his identity, responded to Peter's confession of him as the Christ and experienced the transfiguration.

There are three aspects of this account to concentrate on. First, there is the **affirmation** that we are first and foremost sent out by Jesus into his mission field.

After this the Lord appointed seventy-two others and sent them two by two ahead of him to every town and place where he was about to go. **Luke 10:1**

This calling to be mission minded comes again in the Great Commission, and again in his final words to his infant church in Acts 1:8, not to mention his whole life example. It is essential that we as coaches remember that mission is at the centre of our attention. The

34

missional leaders we coach were created to follow their calling, and as such the only way a coach can help unlock potential is to steer constantly in this direction. A pioneer leader's gifts and skills will not be put to best use unless in a missionary context, nor will their sense of vision, nor will they see anything like the same fruit. The first question for a coach is always, 'Is this leader allowing themselves to be sent by Jesus in this circumstance?'

The second aspect is the *instruction* that Jesus gives. He does not just give them their call and send them out. He follows this up with clear instruction of the steps to take. Note he does not take the steps with them – this is not Jesus the model, this is Jesus the coach. He sits them down and reviews their task... what steps must they take? How can his experience, wisdom and different perspective help them to be successful in what they are about to do? Based on this he gives them instruction...

- Do not take a purse or bag or sandals (v4)
- Do not greet anyone on the road (v4)
- When you enter a house first say, 'Peace to this house.' (v5)
- Stay in that house – do not move around (v7)
- Eat and drink whatever they give you (v7 and 8)
- Heal the sick (v9)
- Tell them, 'The Kingdom of God is near you.' (v9)
- If you are not welcomed wipe off the dust on your feet against them (v10-11)
- Remember that He who listens to you listens to me (v16)... in other words keep a right sense of perspective. Look for what is actually going on, not just what it looks like.

These are all instructions that Jesus could give based on his experience, and when the seventy-two return it is clear that the instruction was both well given and well taken. The fruit that results from the missionary expedition is clearly put down to the strength of instruction the seventy-two were sent with, as well as their obedience and commitment to follow through with what their coach has suggested.

This leads us to our third aspect to concentrate on. Having sent them out with their instruction and seen them return Jesus moves into a time of **review and accountability**. The seventy-two are given space to report back on what they have experienced and express their sense of excitement. Jesus shares their joy, affirming the encouragements, justifying their sense of success:

> *I saw Satan fall like lightning from heaven. I have given you authority to trample on snakes and scorpions and to overcome all the power of the enemy.* **Luke 10:19**

However, he does not leave it at this. The coaching process is not just about sharing in the joys. It is also about assessing their success and looking for the next lessons to learn, the next steps to take, in order to ensure continued growth in their faith and mission experience. Jesus rejoices with them, but also challenges them:

> *However, do not rejoice that the spirits submit to you, but rejoice that your names are written in heaven.* **Luke 10:20**

Jesus draws out that they are still observing what has happened from the wrong perspective. They still have more to learn about whose mission it is and whose power it is. Jesus points their success back to God and encourages them to keep their focus on heaven in all they do. Again, a key question for all coaches, in addition to keeping the missionary focus – is the leader holding the correct perspective?

We can find similar examples of this type of review elsewhere in Jesus' ministry. For example, in Mark 9:14-29 the disciples try and fail to cast out a demon from a possessed boy. Jesus casts the demon out, but more importantly from the coach's point of view he reviews the struggle and failure with the disciples.

He seems almost impatient with them as he has to once again reaffirm a lesson they ought already to have learnt, but he also uses this to teach them something new about the power of prayer and fasting.

We can see that this level of two-tiered accountability is essential in coaching. Not just the missional leader being ready to be honest about their successes and failures, but also the coach being ready to listen to what God is highlighting and prepared to both share the rejoicing and deliver the challenges.

2 TIMOTHY 2:2

This is just a single verse, and as such can only give us a hint of how Paul operated. However, it does seem clear that Paul recognises the importance of a coaching-type system for church leaders. To his protégé Timothy he writes:

And the things you have heard me say in the presence of many witnesses entrust to reliable men who will also be qualified to teach others.
2 Timothy 2:2

What is interesting first is that before we even look at the detail of what Paul is saying, we are drawn to the initial observation that Paul is coaching Timothy here. This becomes increasingly clear as we read the rest of the letter, as well as Paul's previous letter, 1 Timothy. He has taken Timothy under his wing and is offering his experience and perspective to help equip Timothy for his ministry.

We then look at the detail of this verse in particular and we see Paul directly addressing the value of having leaders who oversee others, who in turn oversee others - each passing on their wisdom and experience. And we see that he has identified Timothy as one such leader. In this context this verse becomes a fascinating insight into how Paul invested in those he had identified as following in his ministry, and expected them to mentor and coach others. Again this demonstrates that coaching was a valued practice in the early church, and one that Paul wanted to see passed on and grow as the church spread across the world.

SEEING IT IN ACTION

As we read through the book of Acts we can see this value of coaching in action. If we home in specifically on the account that leads up to and includes Paul's first missionary journey then we can see at least two distinct coaching relationships taking place:

THE BIBLICAL BASIS

1. Barnabas Coaches Saul
(Acts 11:25 - 14:28)

The relationship between Barnabas and Paul (then Saul) begins some time after Saul's vision of Jesus, when Saul wants to meet with the twelve in Jerusalem. It is Barnabas, already by that point a notable member of the Jerusalem church (as we read in Acts 4:36), who speaks on Saul's behalf and bridges the gap between him and the understandably cautious church. Saul is then sent to Tarsus and is out of the story again until Barnabas is sent to Antioch.

Upon seeing that there is a work to be done, he immediately thinks of Saul and brings him in from Tarsus. Barnabas invites Saul to share in his ministry, and consequently Saul joins him in all he does until the end of the first missionary journey.

As this relationship develops we see Saul go through the stages of the discipleship square, as mentioned in chapter one, until Paul is sufficiently mature in his leadership to take over from Barnabas. So when they set out from Antioch the bible always refers to 'Barnabas and Saul', it is Barnabas doing the talking, it is Barnabas that is identified as Zeus by the Gentile Greeks, leaving Saul as Hermes, Zeus' messenger (Acts 14:12).

However, part way through the journey things begin to change. Saul becomes Paul, and from then the bible lists them as 'Paul and Barnabas', and it seems to be Paul doing most of the talking. We observe that one facet of the coaching quality is an openness and joy to see the one they facilitate going further than they ever could.

By the time they return to Antioch they are equals, and when it comes to the second missionary journey Paul is ready to set out on his own, coaching a new team, whilst Barnabas takes John Mark aside, presumably to go through a new coaching process with him. Certainly the next time we hear of Mark he is working alongside Peter, the leader of the church, and then later he is with back with Paul, the man who had originally so objected to him! [8]

2. Paul coaches Silas, Timothy and others
(Acts 15:40 – ch.16 and then into the 2nd and 3rd missionary journeys)

Once Barnabas and Paul have gone their separate ways we see Paul modelling what he has learnt from Barnabas with a new generation of younger leaders. Silas is the first to be taken on board, followed by Timothy and probably Luke. As we read through Paul's letters and the rest of the book of Acts other names crop up and we can see Paul regularly drawing less experienced leaders-in-the-making alongside him so that he can help them reach their potential in their missionary calling.

BIBLICAL VALUES OF COACHING

Having seen how Paul raised the importance of this coaching-type relationship with Timothy, and how he had already modelled this with a variety of leaders

---

[8] More details on the coaching relationship and process between Barnabas and Paul in Antioch and across the first missionary journey can be found in Freddy Hedley's book, *Lessons from Antioch*, published by Emblem, 2007.

based on what he had learned from Barnabas, we also have instances where he spoke more directly of what is expected of the coach. He addresses this particularly clearly in his second letter to the Thessalonians:

> *For you know that we dealt with each of you as a father deals with his own children, encouraging, comforting and urging you to live lives worthy of God, who calls you into his kingdom and glory.* **1 Thessalonians 2:11-12**

These two verses in Paul's letter of instruction give us three key coaching verbs, and they are all in the context of the God who calls you:

- Encouraging – 'yes you can!'
- Comforting – 'yes you will!'
- Urging – 'yes you must!'

So right from the early church we can see some very familiar values in place. Encouraging leaders to see where God is already at work, comforting where leaders are struggling, delivering the challenges and vision of a kingdom-focused life and expecting it to impact on the experience of the leader and mission initiative.

This motif of drawing alongside to give instruction, encouragement, challenge and accountability can be seen time and time again all the way through the bible – not just in the early church. But even the brief examples we have explored here demonstrate how important this role has always been to the growth and success of God's mission and church. And they give a biblical insight into many of the key aspects of coaching that we are now going to unpack through the rest of this book.

YOUR NOTES ON THE CHAPTER...

3

WHAT MAKES A GOOD COACH?

Coaching is a process that relies on the people involved. It is not enough to think that there is a procedure to follow that can guide anyone into being a successful coach. We have already stressed that this is a process based primarily on a relationship. So the role of coach is more than someone who can go through the prescribed motions. Not everyone will make an effective coach.

> *If you want a sneak preview of our top five qualities for missional coaches, you can look at the conclusion in chapter ten.*

Certainly there are a whole range of skills that are necessary and many of these can be learned. However, just as important are the attitude and character of the coach, which are central to coaching effectiveness. Experience also plays a significant part[9]. As we explore what makes a good coach, let us begin with this last point.

---

[9] A group representing Fresh Expressions, Church Army and Churches together in Britain & Ireland is reviewing the related roles of coaching, mentoring, accompaniment and spiritual direction with a view to identifying the core requirements of character and competency. The work in progress document that they have so far developed is reproduced in Appendix III. Their findings helpfully confirm and complement what we describe in this chapter.

EXPERIENCE

In order to avoid the default of falling back on rules of procedure and the potential for 'textbook thinking' it is important that the coach has some level of relevant understanding and experience in the field that the missional leader in question is involved in. The best coaching comes from the real-life experience and wisdom of a coach, filtered through the processes of questioning and accountability. This does not necessarily mean the coach needs to be in a position of recognised leadership or have twenty years hardened church planting under their belt (though they may make an excellent candidate!).

It is also important to focus on the word 'relevant.' There are many church leaders who are gifted and wise, but would be ill-equipped to coach missional leaders as their life-experience simply hasn't taken them in that direction. Consequently they may pour in opposing values, ill-judged advice based on shallow understanding of the issues and be preoccupied with different priorities.

Even leaders with deep experience of a single successful mission project can be too fixed on that model, whereas good coaches are familiar with many models and approaches. And crucially, they appreciate the principles behind each that determine their fruitfulness in their particular context.

A coach should hold the respect of the missional leader, both in terms of the weight of what they can impart and the relevance of it, coming from a shared heart and shared values. But the good coach is aware that experience can limit as well as facilitate. So the character and qualities of the coach are absolutely vital.

We want to emphasise that even before experience, should come the consideration of the crucial attitudes that most contribute to the effective coach.

ATTITUDE

Here we shall consider a range of attitudes that the coach should bring to the relationship. A good coach needs to have a positive attitude towards the leader they are coaching, as well as high expectations of both the process and the potential progress of the leader. A strong coaching attitude tends to be displayed when there are particular assumptions in place. This may not be an exhaustive list, but we would suggest that some of the key assumptions include the following:

Believing in them

We have already covered this briefly in chapter one as a question the coach must ask themselves before agreeing to work with any missional leader. Do I believe in this person? Do I have faith in their vision, their heart, their character and their commitment to see it through? It is essential that the coach has faith in those they coach, and that they are confident in their call. They will need to be positive and affirming at all times, not out of duty, but out of genuine conviction. They should recognise the gifts that God has given those they coach and be quick to draw on these both for encouragement and direction.

But this is not just about choosing the coachee, there is an attitude of good coaches that is positive, that looks for solutions, believes in people and has faith that there is a way through since 'when God calls, he equips'[10].

---

[10] 1 Thessalonians 5:24 & Hebrews 13:21

It's God's mission

An effective coach recognises that it is not about them bringing God with them into the situation, but that God is already there. After all, it is God's mission to the world that we are a part of and the leaders we coach should have that sense that they have been called by God to where He has already begun to work. It is not a coach's job to bring God's approval or presence, but to help discern where God is already at work.

Consequently the coach should come with the readiness and expectation of being surprised and excited by where they find God at work, and a willingness to learn new principles or methods. This understanding that it's God's mission, and therefore on His terms, should also fuel the coach's faith that if they believe the call is correct then there will always be a way through even the toughest ground. This further affirms the coach's role being primarily one of discernment and shared journey over 'external expert'.

It may not be like anything I've done or seen

As we have just asserted, coaches need to be ready to find God in new and unexpected places. As such they need to assume that the vision may involve a range of differences from anything they have encountered before. These might include models of church, tradition and theology, culture and context, leadership style and personality, team dynamics, or even the mission face of the fresh expression. There are no rules or 'blueprints.' There may be common principles and the lessons learned from experience, but the art of coaching is to put these through a filter of discernment and being ready for God to teach new ways.

In terms of attitude there are three key requirements we can draw out from this one assumption. Firstly, there needs to be a degree of humility - an acceptance that 'other approaches can be better than mine'. Secondly, there needs to be a genuine openness. A good coach carries an attitude of 'there is so much we've not yet seen'. And thirdly, a coach needs to not feel easily threatened. They need to understand that different doesn't mean better.

With the Holy Spirit, there's wisdom among us

The next assumption we would highlight is a confidence that with the Holy Spirit involved, there is always access to God's wisdom. Similar to an understanding of it being God's mission, this assumption carries with it an expectation of God's involvement and faith that He will provide guidance and opportunities for growth. This wisdom will come out through discussion, questioning and prayer. So as well as continuous awareness of this 'God dimension', the coach should look for appropriate opportunities to stop and listen.

This sort of enrichment is particularly facilitated by interaction. So it will also come out through the experience of both the coach and the missional leader, which can help directly or be re-interpreted as God brings direct revelation and insights, and hidden things become clear. This can be a particularly dynamic part of the discerning process when in a group coaching situation, or when coupling coaching with involvement in Learning Networks[11].

---

[11] For more information on Learning Networks, including how to get involved in them, see the Fresh Expressions *Share* website at www.sharetheguide.org and also the last section of chapter 8.

I'm not looking to get anything out of this myself

The attitude of humility is linked to a servant attitude. The coach needs to approach the relationship and coaching process with the assumption and intention that all the resulting benefit will be for the project leader and the project. If they have any sense that they are looking to gain from their coaching, then it will take the focus off the pioneer and process and onto themselves.

Unless the coach is clear from the outset that all their orientation is a selfless focus, it is easy for thoughts to creep in, such as, 'How does this affect me or help my agendas?' Having said this, the coach inevitably does gain significantly from exposure to other leaders and projects which expand their learning, but it must be received as a by-product and gratuitous blessing.

Be familiar with principles of mission and leadership, and aware of the current project stage

It is essential that a coach assumes the importance of established principles of mission and leadership that have been learned through their own and others' experience. A large part of the coaching relationship is the opportunity for God to use this independent experience and perspective to inform and challenge. Consequently, a good coach will not only have a clear understanding of what they have learnt, but will also have a knowledge and understanding of some of the key principles that have been learned elsewhere. We will come back to this in later chapters and in Appendix I we specifically include an overview of principles of fresh expressions and church planting.

It is also important that a coach measures the missional leader and the consequential fresh expression against this understanding in terms of what stage they are at, as this will affect what next steps the coach is looking for. It will also give a good gauge of speed of progress, which may again inform the coach of the level of reasonable expectation, or of the level of challenge necessary.

Clear expectations avoid disappointment

It is essential that from the start there is complete openness and honesty about what the aims and expectations of the coaching process are. This can include what will be done, how often, to what end, what are the core values and what level of permission is given to speak into the missional leader's life, ministry and aspirations. This agreement forms a 'Coaching Contract', which it may even be wise to write down in some form, so that it is absolutely understood what the parameters of the relationship are, and it becomes something that can always be returned to.

SKILLS

There are many skills that may contribute to a healthy coaching relationship. The coach's own particular skills and gifts help to build a unique dynamic of coaching, as they bring their own strengths and processes of discernment. However, in addition to what each coach brings of themselves, there are some basic skills that either need to be in place or be learned before one is ready to be an effective coach. These skills include:

- **Being a good listener**
- **Asking good and powerful questions**
- Building faith and confidence through encouragement
- An ability to discern principles from packages
- An ability to hold and apply a complex matrix of leadership and mission principles
- Creating an environment in which to hear God
- Facilitating moving towards plans and action

The first two in this list of skills we have put in bold as these are generic to all coaching and mentoring and underlie all the others.

ROLES OF A MISSIONAL LEADER COACH

Each of these skills is essential for the coaching process to fulfil its potential. In the next chapter we will begin to see how they are used, but let us first consider why these skills are essential by looking closer at a number of roles that the coach may take.

Catalyst / Thought Provoker

The primary aim for any coach is for the missional leaders concerned to grow, both personally and in their ministry, and for them to own their project and ideas. Therefore the coach is there to help stimulate the leader to think and act for themselves. They should pose questions that provoke gut-level answers and then reflect back on these so that the leader is challenged to evaluate their successes, failures, plans and attitudes in order to move forwards.

It can sometimes be easy for the coach to take over in this situation, as they see how their ideas and observations can solve problems or take initiatives to the next level. This must be guarded against. **The coach is never to think for the leader.** This creates dependency and not release, and it can only ever produce short-term outcomes. Part of the discipline of coaching is knowing when to hold back out of an understanding that you are ultimately not a direct part of the mission initiative or fresh expression concerned.

With this in mind, what are the types of questions that missional leaders should be encouraged to be asking and becoming equipped to answer? Some key questions would be:

- Who has God called me to be?
- What kind of church is God calling me to build?
- What mission engagement is God encouraging me into?
- Who is God giving me to work with?
- What things are most important to me (values and priorities)?
- What are my dominant feelings?
- What challenges need facing right now?

Take special note that all of these questions address areas where the pioneer leader has to come entirely to their own conclusion. The coach's questions can help uncover but are never the answer.

Enlightener / Awareness raiser

It is the role of a coach to help the missional leader see what they are not seeing, and to raise awareness levels on anything relevant to the situation. Remember, this is not done by thinking for them, so it is quite a skilful process of questioning and shared exploration and discernment (we will look more closely at how this can be achieved in chapter five). In particular the coach is responsible for helping the leader in their awareness levels.

John Whitmore, in his book *Coaching for Performance*, highlighted the importance and vitality of awareness by saying:

> *I am able to control only that which I am aware of. That which I am unaware of controls me. Awareness empowers me[12].*

Awareness is so important because it enables the leader to address the underlying causes rather than stay at the level of superficially responding to symptoms. The best way of gaining an awareness of what is really going on in any situation is through revelation brought by God. This can come prayerfully, through discussion and challenge or through instinct and sensing. It is part of the coaching role to help the leader listen for this revelation and so raise awareness levels on anything to do with the leader or their mission project.

However, there is also another dynamic of being able to listen to the leader and recognise issues of importance because of the different perspective and experience brought by the coach. One tool that has been developed that can help us understand these different potential areas for awareness raising is the Johari Window[13]. This

---

[12] John Whitman, *Coaching for Performance: Growing People, Performance and Purpose*, 3rd edition, Nicholas Brealy Publishing Ltd, 2002.
[13] Luft, J. & Ingham, H, *The Johari window, a graphic model of interpersonal awareness*, UCLA, 1955.

was first developed in 1955 by two psychologists in the United States, Joseph Luft and Harry Ingham, as a tool for better understanding how relationships work. An example of a blank Johari Window can be seen below.

The Johari Window

	Known to self	Not known to self
Known to others	**Arena**	**Blind spot**
Not known to others	**Façade**	**Unknown**

This is generally used for analysing personal qualities. So a person would choose six adjectives about themselves from a list of 55, as would several of their peers. Adjectives chosen by both the subject and their peers are entered into the **Arena** square – qualities that all are aware of. Adjectives chosen only by the subject are put in the **Façade** square.

This represents information that the subject is challenged to consider whether they should release. Adjectives chosen only by peers are put into the **Blind**

Spot square, as these are traits that the subject may not have spotted in themselves and can only be unearthed by others. The remaining unselected adjectives are added to the **Unknown** square.

This is a tool that can be used as an aid in coaching as it is and could be used to explore issues related to the missional leader, their situation or of the project. However, we also find it useful to apply it to help visualise the coach's role in raising awareness.

The Johari Window below has been filled in from the perspective of where awareness of issues can best be gleaned from. We can see here that the coaching relationship is a crucial part of this awareness developing, as the coach can enlighten the pioneer with things only they see (top right square), but the coach can also facilitate a process that brings God's revelation of what neither of them could see (bottom right square).

Where does the Coach Fit?

	Known to self	Not known to self
Known to others	**Team** *Arena*	**Coach** *Blind spot*
Not known to others	**Individual** *Façade*	**God's revelation** *Unknown*

54

With these two in place, awareness is covered in the whole window. Without either, there is a highly increased potential for blind spots to emerge. We can also see how the coach can have a positive influence on the other two squares as well, by contributing to the Arena square and testing/weighing the results from the Façade square.

So, if this is where the coach fits into the unlocking of awareness, the next question is naturally, 'awareness of what?' The answer to this can include: what is going well (and why), what is going badly (and why), what God is saying and where He is leading. Every leader has blind spots that can often be highlighted best by others with a more detached perspective. Consequently, a coach can play a vital role in helping bring awareness to these by asking searching questions. These questions might relate to areas such as:

- Potential leaders
- Reading the culture
- The leader's own strengths and weaknesses
- Potential blind spots to spiritual hindrances

Affirmer / encourager

The role of affirmer and encourager will be one of the most regularly visited and deeply appreciated roles of any coach. Steve Nicholson, in the *Vineyard Manual of Coaching for Church Planting*, describes it as the 'cheerleaders' and makes the widely recognised point that pioneers often experience a sense of isolation. Pushing the boundaries and taking new territory is not only demanding but can feel like a lonely road. This in part may come about through not being fully understood by the majority of peers in ministry. So the coach will come alongside and can often bring the sort of relief that may be accompanied by a sigh and, 'At least I'm understood.'

A good coach will use affirmation in a number of ways, including:

- Highlighting where God is at work
- Dealing with a leader's sense of isolation
- Strengthening boldness to take risks
- Countering inevitable discouragement
- Affirming levels of commitment and drive
- Sharing successes to rejoice together
- Helping to handle failures
- Building confidence and raising faith
- Alerting the leader to issues that genuinely warrant praise
- Creating a sense of being understood
- Reminding of vision
- Challenging new direction

Advisor

A coach is not only a listener, discerner and encourager. They are also an advisor. This role will normally be in response to the leader asking a question and it is the role where most care is exercised. This does not mean taking on a role of 'outside expert' where you take the helm and effectively make decisions on their behalf, thereby fostering dependency. It does involve drawing on your experience and expertise, and sharing your thoughts and examples where things have worked elsewhere. It may also involve focusing your questions in a particular direction, and being ready to remind the missional leader of the underlying principles of what is being addressed.

Answering questions and offering solutions to problems can sometimes be the right thing to do, but should be done in an open-ended manner that is clearly non-directive. So when suggesting what has worked for you or for others, you may start advice with, 'One option might be...' and so on. Giving models, examples and possible scenarios can be the most helpful way of doing this. Often a leader can answer their own questions if they are posed about someone or somewhere else, so that they are offered that much needed outside perspective. And the coach reflecting back what they hear can lead to the coachee developing their own answers.

Networker/Resourcer

A coach is an important link between the leader and other church plants, fresh expressions or mission initiatives and contacts that have a similar heart and relevant experience. The coach is able to connect the leader to such people who can share ideas and lessons they have learned. They will also point them to the resources they need to progress and will recommend courses, study, reading, retreat and other forms of training and growth.

As Learning Networks (see chapter eight), are developed particularly among fresh expressions leaders, this will become an increasingly accessible option for coaches to point leaders towards. They link them with numerous other leaders who share the same passions and values, and they enable learning to continue as the leaders all input into one another's context from their own experience.

Challenger/Confronter

This may be more of an occasional role, as opposed to the more frequent encouragement and affirmation. However, it is still a very important aspect of the coaching process and means it is essential to have an agreed level of permission to confront as well as affirm. When challenge is called for it should be done clearly but sensitively, and always with prayer included. If avoided through fear, this can build up weaknesses that can undermine the foundations.

Observer

Finally, a coach needs to be an observer. This can and often will be done from a distance and based on what you are told, but ultimately there is nothing like a planned visit – whether that is to their mission context, their public gathering or to their team or leadership meetings. The more you can experience the better informed you will be and the greater depth of understanding you will have. Being able to observe the fresh expression/mission initiative in context can also fuel more penetrating questions and help you give much more detailed feedback in coaching sessions.

These, then, make up the role of the coach. When added to the qualities and skills mentioned before, we now have a detailed measure of what makes a good coach. The next thing to consider is, once you have agreed to coach a missional leader, what does the process involve? The rest of this book will endeavour to unpack this.

YOUR NOTES ON THE CHAPTER...

4

PROCESSES OF LEARNING

If coaching is primarily supporting and enabling a learning process, then it is important that we begin our look at how to coach missional leaders by building an understanding of how people learn. Without this basic understanding it will not matter how skilled the coach is, they will always be missing a key weapon from their armoury. We need to consider both the different ways we learn and what frameworks we can use to best release the learning process.

HOW DO PEOPLE LEARN?

When student teachers are learning how to teach in schools they are trained to plan their lessons around three distinct forms of learning: visual, auditory and kinaesthetic. Put simply: see, hear, do. This is based on established psychological research known as Neuro-linguistic Programming (NLP), or more commonly Sensory Modalities, which highlight the way in which the human brain processes information. These are, we are reliably informed, the different ways in which we all learn[14]. In some areas of teacher training a fourth - oral

---

[14] This research has been published and discussed many times, but for a basic introduction to the main principles, read Joseph O'Connor & John Seymour, *Introducing NLP*, HarperCollins, 1990.

learning - is added as an extension of the auditory, to particularly make the point that we don't just learn by listening to other people's voices, but also our own!

We all rely on all four forms of learning, but for each one of us there will be one or two that stand out more than the others, which we prefer to utilise in order to really embed something in our consciousness. Let's take a few moments to briefly explore each of these forms a little closer:

Visual Learning

We learn through what we see. When I (Freddy) was seven years old, I was stung by a bee for the very first time. It happened by a canal in Windsor whilst my younger brother Nick and I were staying with our grandparents. Nick had never experienced bee stings either, and wasn't even really aware that a bee could cause pain. Watching me writhe in agony (I may have over-reacted a little) was enough for him to learn that he didn't want to ever be stung by a bee himself.

He could *see* that it was best avoided. In schools we see what is written on the blackboard, we watch the teachers' demonstrations, we read information from textbooks. As babies we learn to speak by watching our mother's face and copying the lip movement, as well as observing body language – the word *good*, attached to a smile, must be a positive thing, and so forth. In life we watch other people's reactions; we observe the world around us. In faith we learn that Jesus changes lives by watching it happen in others, we learn how he works in our own life by observing the challenges and encouragements around us.

Auditory Learning

We learn through what we hear. A major part of my brother learning that bee stings involved pain was the sound I made. He recognised it was not the sound of harmony and bliss, but rather pain and desperation. In schools we learn by listening to the teacher. In church we learn by listening to the sermon. In life we learn by listening to the wisdom of others. In faith we learn by listening to God's Word spoken as well as written.

Oral Learning

We learn through what we say. This is an extension of auditory learning, but can in itself operate as quite a distinct learning process. It is an important extension of auditory learning because we don't learn only by hearing other people's voices, but also our own. In schools this is often expressed through question and answer, reading aloud and recital (in languages, drama, even times-tables!). Actors often learn their lines through repeating them over and over until they become second nature. In church we learn our core commitments through declarations and liturgy. How much people learn in this way depends a lot on their personality. The more extrovert among us will rely quite heavily on oral learning, whereas more introverted people may work more through auditory learning.

Kinaesthetic Learning

We learn through what we touch and what we do. On the day I was stung by that bee, we have seen how my brother learnt some important visual and auditory lessons. I, on the other hand, had a kinaesthetic learning experience. I learnt not to squash bees with my bare hands, because it really hurts.

This is not a lesson I could have learned quite as well without doing it, without physically touching the less friendly end of a less than happy bee. Kinaesthetic learning is often the process that sticks with us the longest, and is being increasingly focused on in schools as the best way of teaching a broad range of abilities at once. Nothing bites as hard as experience. Several years after my bee sting, my brother had forgotten some of his lessons that day, and it took a further kinaesthetic experience of his own before he fully learnt to avoid bees at close quarters.

In addition to these four, it may be important to consider a fifth process of learning for the purposes of learning through faith.

Prophetic/Instinctive Learning

We learn through God's Spirit speaking to our hearts. This may be expressed through in-built senses such as perception and instinct, or as a more prophetic sense of God's leading. This obviously falls outside the boundary of psychological analysis but is enormously important as we think about how we learn from experience and principles in a faith context. Some of us will rely more on perception and instinct than others in the way we have been built, but we all need God's guidance in whatever form we sense it, if we are to learn effectively.

Over the years there has been criticism of the way we teach in schools, claiming that we rely too much on the visual and auditory forms of learning. Quite often these are skills that are reasonably well honed in people, but this is mostly due to patterns of nurture, which rarely give the opportunity to learn in different ways. Educational research has suggested that a kinaesthetic approach is actually a much better basis for learning, as a broader range of people responds well to it. Not because the visual and auditory are not vital, but rather because it simply doesn't represent the best needs of many students to use them as the only strategy. A similar focus has been drawn to increasing opportunities for oral learning.

It is important that we do not fall into the same trap when coaching others. If we are going to help missional leaders learn from their experience for their future success, then we need to be aware of the preferred learning methods for that person, but also to expand their learning experiences.

Most of us will be familiar with a church culture that relies heavily on auditory and oral learning – we listen to sermons, recite liturgy, and so on – but the missional leaders we coach may respond better to the visual – being challenged to observe what they see God doing – or the kinaesthetic - exploring the nitty-gritty of their hands-on experience. And certainly we must always look to the prophetic and invite God to speak directly through prayer, prophecy, sensing, instincts and other people.

If we learn through seeing, hearing, doing, saying and sensing, then the coaching relationship needs to cover all of these to fully explore what God is wanting to teach.

THREE INTEGRATED PROCESSES OF LEARNING

We have already considered in chapter one that one of the primary reasons that coaching is important is that it models well what is known as *non-formal learning*. This forms one of three integrated processes or pathways of learning that are generally used in the fields of education and work, and which human experience has shown us cover the different ways that each of us learn through life. In addition to non-formal learning the other two processes are *formal learning* and *socialisation*. Let us look a little closer at each of them.

The characteristic that is written along each side of the triangle, is shared by the two learning processes at either end of that side. Whereas the process at the opposite corner linked by the arrow, has the opposite character. Thus socialisation learning is unintentional although practical and reinforcing traditions. Non-formal is also practically based but follows intentional processes that open to non-traditional outcomes.

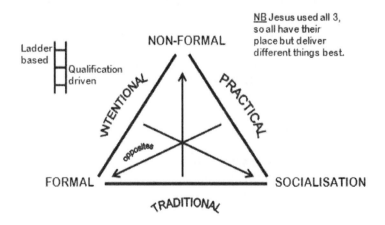

Formal Learning

This is perhaps best expressed in the academic world and western education system. The focus is on the processing of information to demonstrate competence and is often worked out through traditional teaching styles and research, and is usually measured through exams, essays, academic papers and the pursuit of qualifications.

Most formal education is 'ladder-based' in the sense that your learning is organised and systematised so that you move to higher levels of understanding that are based on the previous 'rung'. Principles of algebra depend on more elementary arithmetic, etc.

Formal learning excellently instils an ordered understanding of an area and its concepts, whilst also developing the powers of analysis. As the triangle diagram shows, rather than being based on immediate practical needs and application, it follows intentional programmes and a fixed syllabus and tends to reinforce traditional norms. The products of most theological colleges prove this strength, which can also be a weakness. Formal Learning is extremely valuable in the church as it is an excellent format for all sorts of conceptual understanding, biblical literacy and the ability to think in biblical and ethical ways.

Non-formal Learning

This pattern of learning has been largely neglected in the church. It shares with formal learning the fact that it is an intentional, planned process of growth. But in complete contrast the plans for learning are built around undertaking a practical enterprise such as building, carpentry, and until recently, nursing. The practicalities of the tasks set the agenda for the learning. Non-formal learning is also more personally tailored. The individual abilities and needs of the trainee in their vocation and assignments can also define how the learning takes place and skills are learned through a mixture of principles, experience, modelling and coaching.

The most prominent form of Non-formal Learning has probably been the apprentice system that is now making a comeback in the workplace. Another example would be the first century Jewish of disciples attaching themselves to live alongside a Rabbi. And as we have already pointed out, this process of learning has a direct relationship to coaching in terms of helping leaders learn the skills they need to follow their calling.

Socialisation

If formal and non-formal learning are the options available for an intentional process, then socialisation covers all the learning that happens as a result of the everyday, unplanned, random, practical experience without training. The University of Life is how some might call it, and we've all met people who left school at fifteen and made their own way in the world, becoming successful after years of toil and learning the hard way.

But even more importantly, almost all our learning in our early years comes through socialisation in our family and neighbourhood. This is unplanned but most profound as we learn everything from how to eat with a knife and fork to our complete competence in our native language. And even more important is that socialisation lays the foundation for our worldview, values and behaviour – building most of our culture and tradition. This also applies to our socialisation learning through our experience of church. And this unplanned, unconscious learning is the hardest to shift!

In a general sense, the trick is to learn how we best learn and which form of learning applies best to which situations and desired outcomes. We will all have a process of learning that suits us best, but we are unlikely to learn best without a mix of all three – but it helps if they are implemented in the right places at the right times.

By definition, missional leaders will spend most of their time out in the world and so will be constantly going through a process of socialisation learning. However, formal learning can provide a vital background framework in that context, and non-formal learning can help make sense of what is being experienced in the field. When applied in this way, coaching can be a powerful process and an important bridge between formal and socialised learning.

However, there are two extremely important specific conclusions for our purposes, which come from the understanding of these three distinct processes of learning. First is the recognition that the instincts and principles of missional church are most readily acquired through being socialised in a missional church context. Missional church is a corporate social enterprise and hence most of the lessons are best learnt by immersion in a good example of such a community. And because socialisation learning is unplanned and goes very deep, it takes a significant length of time.

The second vital recognition is that missional leadership is best learnt through non-formal processes. And first and foremost, these happen when being apprenticed to and working alongside a gifted and experienced pioneer. Then when ready to lead a mission project themselves, the ongoing learning is best facilitated by coaching and a peer-learning network.

It is so important that the coach appreciates the different parts that these processes play. This will enable them to both see how their contribution fits and can be most effective, but also helps them recognise the right training and experience needs of the pioneer missional leader.

A FRAMEWORK TO USE

As we develop our understanding of how we learn, we also need to consider what frameworks we can use as coaches to help us, together with our coachees, to recognise and process what we are learning. There are numerous frameworks used by different churches and coaches across the world, and you may well have one of your own that you prefer. For us, we would like to draw your attention to the Learning Circle, which forms part of the LifeShapes teaching developed at St Thomas' Church, Sheffield[15].

The Learning Circle

This has been developed by Mike Breen from more familiar forms such as the world mission learning circle

---

[15] As mentioned earlier, LifeShapes been published more fully in *The Passionate Church* and *A Passionate Life*, both written by Mike Breen and Walt Kallestad and published by Nexgen (2004 and 2005 respectively).

(observe, reflect, act) and the pastoral cycle (experience, reflection, action) and is widely used in mission, church and business to help follow a structured rhythm of learning. Mike's expanded version most importantly opens up the cycle to interaction with others and hence also to accountability.

It therefore forms a much more applicable foundation to coaching processes. This *LifeShapes* learning circle is based on Jesus' call for us to live out a life of faith based on learning, as expressed in Mark 1:14-15:

> *After John was put in prison, Jesus went into Galilee, proclaiming the good news of God. 'The time has come,' he said. 'The kingdom of God is near. Repent and believe the good news!'*

As we look at this opening statement and continuing challenge of Christ's ministry we can see it is an invitation to a life of learning. The first thing to note is that those who responded became known as Jesus' disciples. We tend to think of this as meaning a follower, but in fact the word disciple (in Greek this is the word *mathetes*) means 'learner'. Jesus invited people to come and learn from him.

In order to learn from Jesus we need to recognise that the time has come to embrace a life of repentance and belief. The word 'time' (*kairos*) means a specific moment in time or 'event' time, rather than the wider perspective of a span of time or measured time (*chronos*). Repentance (*metanoia*) means to change our mind, and the word 'believe' (*pistis*) means practical trust as we act on our conviction.

So Jesus invites us into a life where we are watching for the specific moments, events and circumstances where we can learn from God, turning away from our own understanding and ways of responding and changing our minds to learn from Christ, and then putting our conviction into action.

LifeShapes has expressed this pattern of life-long learning as a cycle, starting at a significant event or learning opportunity (kairos moment) and then reflecting and learning from that event before deciding on a course of action. To aid the visual learners, this is shown through the diagram below.

The LifeShapes Circle

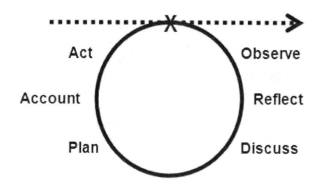

So a framework for learning looks like this: as we move through life (the passing of time – or *chronos* in Greek – is represented by the dotted arrow) we look for the significant moments that stop us in our tracks (*kairos*), seen as an X above. These might be positive or negative, from the birth of a child to the death of a friend, from a Holy Spirit impact moment to difficult setbacks in ministry, from recognising a new opportunity to hitting a barrier to progress.

Once a kairos situation has become clear, we enter into a process of repentance. This works by observing what has happened, reflecting on it and discussing it with others (including prayer). This is for the purpose of gaining God's perspective. It is about looking beyond the surface of an event and searching for what is really happening – where is God in all this? How should I be responding? What are the opportunities for change and growth here?

This done, it is time to take the steps of faith based on what we've heard God say. This is done by making a plan, holding yourself accountable and then acting it out. The focus on this side of the circle is towards basing your faith on action, being ready to act on what you have learned so that those lessons embed themselves in experience. From here you are ready to move forwards again in life, watching for the next kairos moment to learn from, which may be the outcome of your action.

With this framework we can clearly see the coach's participation in this process with the missional leader. The coach's role is to help the missional leader identify their kairos moments, events, opportunities or circumstances. Then to guide them through the stages of repentance (observation and reflection) and faith (planning, accounting and action), and to both hold them accountable for the resulting action taken and to help them reflect further on the outcomes of their decisions.

This is no easy task, especially given that life isn't as orderly as we would like and doesn't come one kairos moment at a time, each waiting for the previous to be dealt with. The first key skill is to help the missional leader separate out their kairos situations and to home in on the ones that are most directly relevant to their calling. Then it is a case of working through them as systematically as can be managed, whilst always being ready to let priorities of life and new experiences reorder the queue.

It can seem daunting and a little systematic to begin with, but once this process is underway it can become much more organic as the circle is negotiated more and more. Eventually it becomes so instinctive that the missional leader will be well equipped to be looking and to recognise kairos moments as they come, and will instinctively know how to grow in their own more intentional learning process.

You should be able to see how the details of the coaching method that we now explore fit with these stages of a learning cycle.

YOUR NOTES ON THE CHAPTER...

5

FRAMEWORKS FOR QUESTIONS

Having explored an understanding of some of the different ways people learn, and considered a basic framework to help work through that learning, the next stage is to look at what the coaching process looks like in practice. In this chapter we want to particularly explore the importance and dynamics of questions.

Although the coaching process does involve lots of observation and reflection on the part of the coach, mostly the job entails channelling these observations and reflections into asking good questions to help the missional leader do their own observation and reflection so that they come to their own conclusions and set their own goals and plans for action. The coach then holds the leader accountable for the outcome and sets in motion the next stage of learning through new questions. So *asking good questions* is one of the two most fundamental skills for a coach.

However, before we think about what sort of questions we should and should not be asking, there is a first step that needs to be in place: that of *listening well*. And this is the other most fundamental coaching skill. Because no question, no matter how relevant, is any good unless the coach has developed the skill of listening. They need to listen first to discern what questions to ask as well as perceptively listening to the answers. So our starting point in considering how to ask good questions is how to listen well.

LISTENING WELL

Most of us are much better at speaking than listening. It's a rare art that needs cultivating and requires practice. And it may well be that especially those of us in church leadership who coach others may have to resist the habit of always doing the talking. If we see coaching as an advisory role we can fall into the trap of speaking too much. Instead we need to recognise the power of listening. Listening is a skill and as such can be learned and honed. To help recognise where we are strong and where we still need to develop these skills, here are some strong do's and don'ts about listening.

Do...

1. Focus on them – look at their eyes: Nothing demonstrates to the speaker that you are listening more than looking them in the eye (but don't stare!). People feel more at ease opening up when they know their contribution is being valued, and when they can see in your eyes that you are not judging them, but there to help.

2. Concentrate intentionally: Don't assume from the start of a sentence that you know where it is going to end. Pay close attention to what is being said, and be listening for what you think God might be revealing.

3. Note their tone of voice: Do they sound relaxed, tense, frustrated, encouraged? Does the tone of their voice match up to the information or answers they are giving? Tone can be an indicator of when people are holding something back – be that through discomfort, shyness or humility. It's thought that 40% of verbal communication is through tone of voice.

4. Be aware of body language: Experts tell us that something like 90% of communication is non-verbal, of which 50% is body-language. So don't assume that all your questions will be answered through their voice.

5. Notice negative words, repetition, contradictions, a shift to formality: These can be clear pointers to things of importance or signs that someone is closing up and putting their defences in place. If noticed early, and permissions have already been agreed in the coaching relationship, then these early signs can be addressed and used to go deeper in positive ways.

6. Identify passions, themes and encouragements: These can provide a really positive context and indicator of what is important and where the leader is being called, and can therefore become a measure for when they are and are not moving forwards. The less they talk about their passions, for example, the harder they may be struggling as their competence has yet to match up to their enthusiasm – revealing a D2 phase of ministry (see the Discipleship square in chapter one).

7. Be sensitive to anything God may highlight: Be praying as you are listening, asking God to reveal what he wants to draw attention to through direct revelation, biblical insight, the wisdom in the room and ideas that emerge through discussion. God may also speak through throw-away comments or some of the indicators above.

8. Be aware of your own filters, passions & issues that affect your objectivity: Inevitably we bring into the coaching relationship our own priorities, the way we think things should be done, and our prejudices. These can be strengths - experience, perspective and wisdom will be a large part of why a coach is chosen – but can also be potential weaknesses if they get in the way of being objective and hearing God speak in new ways. Self-awareness and a willingness to be humble are key to this working.

9. Reflect back to them what you've heard: Reflection and reflective learning are fundamental to good coaching. It's helpful to simply restate what you've heard. You may paraphrase or condense, summarising without changing the meaning. This has three considerable benefits. First, it gives the missional leader the chance to correct areas we have misheard or misunderstood. It also gives the coach a chance to hear the information again, drawing on the oral learning principles from chapter four. And thirdly, it gives the perfect springboard for the next step of discussion as the missional leader reacts to your interpretation of what they have said. Many important lessons are learned simply through this re-iterating from a new perspective, and can often help the leader identify their own strengths and weaknesses as they hear them expressed by someone else.

Don't...

1. Be thinking of what you want to say: If you are concentrating on what you want to say then your attention is not fully on the speaker. It is usually helpful to make notes, both of what they are saying (so you can return to them without fear of missing anything out) and of any thoughts you have (which can be developed in later discussion). In this way you avoid allowing your attention to stray. For more prophetic coaches it may also be that if they hold off on planning their answers, then there is increased opportunity for God to speak directly.

2. *Interrupt:* Interruptions will inevitably take the discussion down tangents that can be explored later, no matter how important. The immediate result is that the missional leader either forgets what they were going to say, or they have an excuse to not address important issues that they were putting off until they reached the 'crescendo' of the problem they are describing.

3. *Pre-plan your questions too much:* It is important to let the missional leader and the general flow of conversation set the main direction. This keeps the coaching process organic and gives it the best possible chance of covering the areas that are most pertinent to the particular leader in question, rather than dealing only in generic issues that are experienced by many, but not all.

4. *Project onto them how you think or act:* This goes for both your positive and negative traits. The missional leader needs to feel they can be themselves and communicate in the way that best suits them. This doesn't mean you have to change your way of processing things, but it does mean don't expect them to do it your way!

ASKING GOOD QUESTIONS

The art of asking good questions is a tricky one. It is easy to ask questions that are not searching enough, out of assumed politeness or reluctance to be too challenging. On the other hand it can also be easy to ask questions that are too challenging at an early stage before trust levels have been sufficiently built. However, if we keep in mind the main aims behind the questions we ask, then we are likely to do much better.

Aims

Good questions are designed to help the leader. This applies to helping them increase his/her awareness level; helping them to think more deeply and helping them examine issues; and then draw principles and ideas from those issues. In this way the leader will grow, develop their own ideas and solutions, and so own responsibility for the project. Such questions also enable the coach to discern where the leader is up to, what the issues in their leadership/life are and how to respond appropriately.

Examples from Coaching Sport

As an illustration of the sort of thing we mean, let us return to the world of coaching in sport that we introduced in chapter one. In particular, let's consider tennis. There will obviously be a lot of time devoted to working on improving particular skills, but the best way to identify the areas that need addressing is to examine performance and get the player to identify where they want and need to develop.

A tennis coach will want to ask questions that:

- Help the player's awareness of their talent and form
- Examine specific areas of weakness
- Identify common trends that can be learned from or need to change
- Encourage the player to think what are the next steps that need to be taken to improve

With this in mind, what sort of questions might the coach be asking? There could be any number, but if you imagine that a player and a coach are in a practice session or watching a replay of the player's last match, then here are a few suggestions of questions that might get asked:

- Which way was that ball spinning as it came to you?
- How high was that ball when it came over the net?
- What was the same about your opponent's last four shots?
- What does that tell you about them?
- When did your opponent show signs of emotional weakness?

You may be able to think of many others, but this opens up for us some general categories of question to look for. They are designed to help the player dig deep and identify their own areas for development. They are specific without being suggestive of 'the answer'; they help the player to see what is important and the things they've missed.

GOOD QUESTIONS

Using the above example, we can draw out some helpful guidelines for what makes a good question in a coaching relationship. The following dos and don'ts are reflected in the suggested tennis coach questions above, and are hopefully also applicable to any questions you thought of yourself.

Do...

1. Ask open questions: These require descriptive, more extensive answers that probe deeper understanding.

2. Use interrogative question words: These include words like *What, When, Who, Where, How often, How many?* These words require the most thought from the missional leader, and give the best chance for unearthing insight and getting to the facts.

3. Lead from the general to the specific: Use follow-on questions to press beyond the superficial. Secondary questions like *What does that tell us?* or *Why do you think that might be?* are good at uncovering further levels of awareness.

4. Allow questions to stay with an area of current importance or of interest to the missional leader: There are so many possible issues that focusing on a few each session can be more effective than ranging too widely.

5. Make your questions practical and not theoretical: Practical questions keep both the coach and the pioneer, focused on the task in hand and reduce the opportunity for getting distracted by unrooted theory.

Don't...

1. Ask many closed questions: These are ones that can be answered by a simple 'Yes' or 'No'. They don't lead anywhere and don't press for deeper thought or analysis. So, for example, questions such as, 'Do you think that went well?' are not as helpful as, 'How do you think that went?'

2. Threaten or imply criticism with your questions: This will make the leader defensive and stifles growth. 'Why?' questions can trigger defensiveness. The same exploration can be achieved by re-phrasing 'Why?' as 'What were the factors/reasons....?'

3. Ask leading questions: These can be spotted by the leader and can seem to manipulate. If the coach has a suggestion or wants to move in a certain direction, its better just to say so.

4. Introduce questions that are digressions or result in side-tracking: As mentioned earlier, if another issue occurs to you before finishing the current exploration, jot it down for later.

Examples

Taking these guidelines into consideration, here are a few sample questions that might be appropriate as starters in coaching situations:

- What plans do you have for team building in the next six months?
- Who are your evangelists and most effective people gatherers?
- What steps are you taking to understand your target community, to discover people's needs, to identify their meeting points and discern the *leading edge of mission*?
- Who are your next level of potential leaders?
- When do you think you will want to multiply the small group?
- How would that leadership/mission principle be interpreted in your context?
- What has God been highlighting or saying to you since we last met?
- Where are you feeling most stress at the moment?
- In what ways does your planned gathering event reflect the preferences of non-church people?

- What steps are you taking to help people find their gifts and use them?

FIVE TYPES OF QUESTION

Now that we have introduced the basics of good questions, let's sharpen our skills by considering some other helpful aspects of enquiry. We have already differentiated between the first two types of question...

1 & 2: Open and Closed Questions

We have already explained this key difference between:
- *Closed questions* – just require yes or no and lead nowhere. Whereas...
- *Open questions* – require explanation and analysis and invite to go deeper.

Along with his co-authors, John Whitmore, in *Co-active Coaching*[16], expands our armoury of questions with these three other categories:

3 & 4: Information Gathering & Curious Questions

Some good questions ensure significant answers beyond yes/no, and they are focused directly on eliciting particular information. These *information gathering questions* have an important part to play in coaching as they gather important facts. Even strictly

---

[16] John Whitmore, Laura Whitworth, Henry Kemsey-House, Phil Sandahl, *Co-active Coaching: New Skills for Coaching People Towards Success in Work and Life*, Davies-Black Publishing, 1998.

non-questions like 'tell me more about your evangelism strategy', invite further details.

However, with our emphasis on raising levels of awareness the fourth category of questions are *curious* or *probing questions*. These, as their names imply, go beyond just establishing facts and press behind the facts to uncover things like motives, issues, possibilities, desired outcomes and explanations. Here are some illustrative examples:

Information Gathering questions	Curious or Probing questions
What questions will you include in the community survey?	What do you want the survey results to give you and to enable you to do?
How much exercise do you need each week?	What would 'being fit' look like for you?
What are the training options available for your team?	How do you want the training to develop those leaders?

5: Empowering Questions

Lastly, Whitworth helpfully distinguishes questions that not only go deeper, but are specifically aimed at giving more control and extending possibilities and options to the pioneer leader.

In the tables above and over the page, we have given examples of the sorts of coaching questions that could fit these categories when coaching missional leaders and those planting fresh expressions of church.

Empowering questions
• What could increase your options for recruiting team?
• How could you regain control in that area? Do you need to?
• What is the fear here that you need to find freedom from?
• How could you make this mission engagement more effective?
• What resources would you need to unlock this limitation?
• What might initiate reconciliation between those team members?
• What steps do you imagine might melt their resistance to change?

INTENTIONAL DISCIPLINED STEPS LEAD TO NATURAL SKILL

For most of us these most important skills of listening and good questions don't come naturally. We have to develop the habits consciously until they are built into our natural responses. This may seem stilted and artificial at first but it's the only way to build learned skills into a lifestyle.

Here again the discipleship square, introduced in chapter one, explains the steps we have to go through to gain any complex ability. Mike Breen has helpfully illustrated this with learning to drive a car. Every teenager, as they contemplate getting behind the wheel for the first time, starts the D1 stage as *unconsciously incompetent*. So too as new coaches we don't yet have any experience of the complex and sophisticated processes of listening and questioning, and are unaware of what we don't know. But as we begin to get involved, the whole range of new dos and don'ts confronts us and we hit D2 and become *consciously incompetent*, like the first few times we actually try to drive the car!

But if we are ready to practice and persevere, however forced it may feel, we grow to D3 when we are becoming *consciously competent*, intentionally thinking through the right listening attitudes and questioning styles and applying as appropriate. Now things begin to be really fruitful in our coaching even though very programmed, like the driver thinking 'mirror, clutch, select gear, engage, release brake, accelerate'.

Then finally comes the bliss of driving without thinking as *unconscious competence* is achieved. In coaching the same result emerges, with instinctive 'discovery listening' and all categories of good questions being asked naturally in the appropriate situations.

The journey through these four stages is essential for the growth of the effective coach if we are to reach this desired goal.

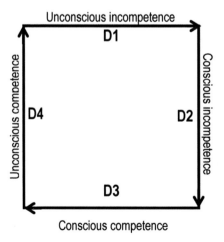

YOUR NOTES ON THE CHAPTER...

6

G.R.O.W.

FOUR STEPS TO BUILD ON GOOD QUESTIONS

Listening well as a foundation for good questioning is very important but good questions are not ends in themselves. As coaches, we want to help missional leaders move from increased awareness to fruitful action. This will involve clarifying aims and goals, reaching decisions and making plans for implementation. This coaching process is commonly arranged around the acronym GROW[17]. which Steve Nicholson and Jeff Bailey of Vineyard, have adapted for coaching church planters and missional leaders, and which breaks down as follows:

- **GOALS:** which need to be the current expression of the vision and purpose of the church, fresh expression or mission initiative.

- **REALITY** checking to objectively assess the present situation.

- **OPTIONS:** to be reviewed as strategies to move from goals to reality.

- **WILL:** the exercising of decisions between options that lead to action.

---

[17] Further details on this coaching framework with suggested questions and downloadable materials can be found at www.janbrause.co.uk. The context of this material is for business coaching, but the principles are essentially the same when applied to mission and church leadership.

This framework not only gives the coach a clear process to follow with missional leaders, but it also offers a wider focus for questions. The order of these steps can vary, especially between **goal setting** and **reality checking**. However, it is usually best not to assess where you are in isolation, but in the light of the current wider goals of the church that the missional leader is at or the fresh expression they are seeking to plant.

This highlights the gap and helps focus on the **options** which will move you from where you are to where you want to get to. Lastly, you can then help the missional leader decide on a plan of action – determining their **will**. Sometimes this framework or sequence will be explicit and other times less obvious. But the recognition of this process will help the leader make it part of their own processing. It is probably helpful to write down these stages as the session progresses or even for the coach to always have them as headings on a blank sheet. Let's look closer at each stage of this GROW process.

GOALS

Start where you want to end up! The best planning starts with your long term aim and works back. The DAWN (Discipling a Whole Nation) strategy of church planting works this way. It asks what would it look like to fulfil the Great Commission in our nation and then works out what might be the necessary steps to get there. This is both biblical and practical. Biblical in that it reflects well the way that Jesus invited people to follow him based on the big picture – 'The kingdom of God is near' - before then taking them on a gradual process of discipleship. Practical in that it gives you a measure with which to gauge progression and growth.

90

G.R.O.W.

This approach to setting goals raises vision and faith and avoids limiting expectations based on past failures or present barriers. It also ensures that short term aims fit the big picture and don't take us off track.

Good Goals are SMART

The Church Growth School, among others, have taught us that many of our goals are woolly and so general that they are almost useless to **motivate** or **monitor** progress. They have given us the acronym SMART to help sharpen up our goal setting. It breaks down as follows:

Specific – Good goals are specific goals, which include relevant detail and particular hopes for the future to enable clear planning and that can be assessed when the time comes. So, for example, an unhelpful goal might be, 'I want more leaders'. It is very difficult to make appropriate and tailored plans for such a non-specific outcome. Also, in a year's time, when there are no new leaders, it's impossible to assess why that is the case; how near to being the case it is; or whether it is ever likely to be the case. All you know is that the goal was not reached. It serves only to discourage. Instead, a much more helpful goal might be, 'To introduce a program to identify potential leaders and establish a two-phase training'. This can then form the basis for developing the best plans for identification and training of the new leaders for the desired projects or ministry areas.

Measurable – Following on from being specific, good goals need to be easily measurable. It is not helpful to set as a goal, 'We want a good number selected and enrolled in the training.' Who is to say what is a good number? However, stating that 'I want 20% of the church membership to have been invited into this training' or 'I want all of the fresh expression team to have enrolled and completed the training', is not only more specific, but is a detail that can be easily revisited.

Agreed – Goals are highly unlikely to be worked towards unless everyone involved takes ownership of them. Everyone needs to want the goal to be reached if they are to be fully motivated to see it happen. Therefore it is essential that all set goals are agreed by all concerned. The coach cannot set goals, and nor can the missional leader. The coaching relationship may well identify desired goals, but these then need to be refined and adopted by the leaders and core team of the fresh expression or mission initiative.

Realistic – It is no good setting goals that are highly unlikely to be achieved. Again, this is only a route to discouragement and loss of confidence in leadership. This does not mean setting easy goals, but rather aiming for what will challenge (or even stretch), but is still a realistic target. So, continuing with our example of raising leaders, whilst we need all the leaders we can get, it may be that a more realistic goal recognises that 'identifying 10% of members' or 'all of the fresh expressions team' is both achievable as well as challenging and inspiring.

Time-framed – It is important to set a time-frame for when goals are hoped to be achieved. Again, this enables them to be used to monitor progress as they are periodically revisited, reviewed and, if necessary, planning adjustments made. So an unhelpful goal would be, 'This could take a while to get established', whereas a more helpful goal might say, 'We will have identified the 10% within six months and started the first phase training in nine months'. Again, this keeps the goals specific and measurable, and enables experience to shape what is realistic.

The difference between broad and strategic goals

Goals can be applied to every area of development and planning, and relate to both the big picture of where we want to progress to, as well as the detailed picture of what that journey looks like step by step. It is therefore important to recognise the difference between *broad* and *strategic* goals.

Broad Goals (or End Goals) relate to the big picture. They are still SMART, but they are broad in scope and are generally less under our direct control. For example, having a goal 'to see 30% of next year's growth through conversions' is a broad goal that is specific, measurable and potentially realistic, but does not deal with any nitty-gritty details of how that might be achieved (always recognising that its achievement will also depend on the direct work of God!). The same might be said of our SMART goal above of having 10% of the church membership selected and in training within nine months.

Strategic Goals, on the other hand, identify the detailed steps that are within our control to give most chance of achieving the end goal. So taking the example where the broad goal is to see 30% of next year's growth through conversions, what might be the strategic goals? Well, they could include the following:

- Train half the church in personal evangelism.
- Organise a mission week and three 'reaping' events linked to current 'sowing'.

- Staff members next year to develop one new relationship with a non-Christian to model evangelistic lifestyles.

These are again all specific and measurable, but are concentrating more on what can be done to work towards the broad goals. You could then take each of these strategic goals and set further strategic goals beneath them, such as covering what a mission week looks like or how it could be organised.

A question to consider

Have a think about the second example of a broad goal that we have raised... seeing 10% of church membership selected and in training for leadership within nine months. What might be some of the strategic goals that compliment this broad goal?

REALITY

An objective exploration of where the mission development, fresh expression or church plant is up to in relation to the vision and goals is essential for the missional leader to develop plans for the way forward. Examining the reality of the situation will mean identifying both things to celebrate and things that challenge. Clearly the celebrations are opportunities to praise and thank God for where He is at work and to be encouraged that there is fruit to be found. This will do wonders for helping the missional leader stay focused in the conviction they are in the right place and will motivate them to press ahead, even in times when encouragements seem thin on the ground.

G.R.O.W.

Starting with the encouragements is important as it sets the tone, and often they are not given enough time as we seek to jump into problem-solving. That being said, honestly facing the gaps is just as important and challenges the missional leader to look for where God is highlighting the need for further development. It also motivates leaders to address the action required. For both the encouragements and the challenges, the attitudes needed here are:

- Objectivity & honesty
- Sensitivity
- Detachment, not criticism or judgement
- Encouragement wherever authentically possible
- Being descriptive not evaluative – say what you see, not why you think you see it.

Again, questions are the key tool so that the missional leader is led to their own assessments. Good linked questions for reality-checking include:

- What steps/action have you taken on this so far?
- What were the effects/outcome of that action?
- What does that tell us about your situation?

Continuing with our theme of helpful acronyms, another well known aid to fully exploring the present reality is a SWOT analysis – assessing Strengths, Weaknesses, Opportunities and Threats. This can be applied to both the individual progress of the leader (strengths being things such as gifts and vision, weaknesses being personal challenges, and so forth), as well as the ongoing development of the fresh expression or mission initiative (what are the strengths of the team; what have been the real encouragements so far; where are the areas you are failing to achieve your goals, etc). Many find this a very helpful and systematic approach and as such some may consider this their preferred tool for assessing the reality of the situation.

OPTIONS

The more options we can identify the better the chance of finding the best course of action. And the clearer the understanding we have gained of the current situation, the more options the planter is likely to identify.

Greenlighting

Options will usually get filtered out in the normal atmosphere of critical evaluation. Discussion does bring up ideas, suggestions and other avenues but by the very nature of the process, evaluation sifts out the 'bad/dangerous ideas' as they emerge and only develops ideas that initially seem to be worth exploring.

The trouble is that often the best options are not immediately obvious, and may not even compliment current understanding of 'good practice'. So often novel or radical ideas never get considered because we think things have to appear sound and safe. In this particular area, the coach has a key role to encourage **quantity** not **quality**.

Greenlighting means intentionally agreeing to suspend practical assessment (showing the red light) and just to generate alternatives. The aim is to draw as many options as possible from the missional leader so as to maximise choices. Common thoughts that can limit options include:

- It can't be done
- It can't be done like that
- They would never agree/let that happen
- It will cost too much
- We can't give it enough time/effort

Greenlighting bypasses these limits by asking 'What if' questions, allowing any number of different ideas to be floated without being shown a red light before proper consideration. So approaches that open the options might include:

- What if ... the finances were there?
- What if ... you had enough people?
- What if ... God did the unexpected?
- What if ... that barrier/problem didn't exist?

Taking a missional leader through this process means encouraging them to think outside the box and throw in any and every option they can think of, no matter how unrealistic it may seem – remember, quantity not quality at this stage. When the leader has exhausted his or her options the coach may also need to be ready to offer more. This is especially likely to be true in the early phases of the coaching relationship.

Furthermore, this practice of encouraging creative imagination is especially appropriate when coaching pioneers in mission because by its very nature this endeavour involves pushing the boundaries.

WILL - DECISION MAKING

Based on the **goals** that have been agreed, an honest assessment of the **reality** of the situation and the **options** that have been identified, the coach then needs to help the missional leader reach a solid decision for the next steps of action to take. Decisions taken need to be clear and the missional leader must be really committed and motivated to see them through. John Whitmore, in his book *Coaching for Performance*, described this stage in the GROW process in this way:

> *... to build an action plan to meet specific requirements, on ground that has been thoroughly surveyed, and using the widest possible choice of building materials.*

Again, in order for coaches to help missional leaders make their own decisions, questions are essential. Clearly, these questions need to be focused on action-specific implementation plans and enable decisions to be taken. The type of questions that might prove helpful could include:

- What are you going to do?
- When are you going to do it?
  Timing is often the issue. The coach may need to help the leader review it and then tie them down!
- Will the chosen course meet your goal?
  If not, should the action shift or the goal be modified?
- What are the possible obstacles to watch for?
- Who needs to be brought in on the decision?
- What support will be needed?

At the end of this sort of decision making should come a crunch question:

- Score 1 to 10 for how certain you are to carry out the agreed action.
  This is a measure of the leader's commitment, not the likely outcome. If the leader scores themselves below 8 out of 10 you can reduce the challenge or lengthen the time frame, if appropriate. Better to delete the action than pile up guilt with incomplete, unrealistic job lists.

ANOTHER WAY TO LOOK AT GROW

There is another way that is used by some coaches to think of and remember exactly this same framework and process as a structure to a session. Whilst starting by clarifying and keeping in mind the current overall objectives (Goals), they proceed to focus on *'what is'* (Reality), then to *'what could be'* (Opportunities) and finally to *'what will be'* (Will). This is unpacked further at the end of chapter eight (p.128-129), when we explore how this structure applies to a particular peer-coaching method.

PRIORITISING THE GROW STEPS

As these GROW steps are applied in coaching it can be helpful, both for planning coaching sessions and evaluating their progress, to have a broad guide to the proportion of emphasis and time commitment given to each step. By far the main focus of the coach should be given to exploring **options** to find solutions, as this is the most important and effective supporting role that the coach brings to those in missional leadership.

We would therefore recommend, as a rule of thumb, the following proportions of time and emphasis given to each step:

Goals - *10%*
Reality - *10%*
Options - *60%*
Will   - *20%*

This is unpacked further, along with examples of sample questions for each of the GROW stages in Appendix III.

OTHER RELATED PROCESSES

There are other coaching methods that have been developed, and most are based on the same basic values. Indeed, many can be used alongside GROW as a complimentary aid to the process. Some of the best examples we know of are:

The Coaching Wheel

This has been used extensively in the Natural Church Development movement and was developed by Bob Logan and Coachnet, so as you might expect it is extremely compatible with GROW This is discussed further in the next chapter.

The COACH model

This model was developed by Keith Webb and CRM Singapore, and is a five-stage process that breaks down as follows:

- *Connect:* The first stage is about having a time of engaging with the coachee, building a rapport and trust within the relationship.
- *Outcomes:* This is about determining the session goal.
- *Awareness:* This involves a time of reflective dialogue, where insights can be shared and explored.
- *Course:* Having spent time exploring these insights the next phase is one of putting them into practical steps.
- *Highlights:* Once this is done it is now time to review all that has emerged and to identify what has been helpful.

The DASA Principle

This is another acronym and describes a process that perfectly fits with GROW and particularly with Goals that are SMART. It stands for *Decide, Act, See what happens, Adjust.* These simple steps used in some coaching, are designed to maximise the freedom to be flexible, on the conviction that the person with most flexibility has most power.

You can see that it starts where GROW ends, with a decision – the will to act. In this sense it completes the circle by examining anything and everything that resulted from the implementation of agreed plans, in order to conclude with a new adjusted Goal. The steps press the coachee to ask, 'What did and didn't work?' in an exploration for all the signs of internal and external change. This enables a dynamic evaluation, enhancing the willingness to adapt as the coachee sees the developing outcomes of action, rather than digging in and expecting others to adjust.

So this DASA framework is a tool that can be taken on by pioneer leaders to use themselves as they implement agreed plans. It also ideally fits at the start of a coaching session as the goals and plans agreed last time are reviewed and processed through to new revised goals in the light of what actually happened.

Transformissional Coaching

This is a term that has been coined in the US by Steve Ogne and Tom Nebel and describes a process that they have developed around seven coaching behaviours[18]. Ian Hamilton, of CRM, describes these behaviours as follows:

- *Listen* empathetically (and carefully) – seek to understand before being understood; use your ears, eyes, questions and the discernment of your heart to enhance this listening.
- *Celebrate* victories – ensuring that the focus of coaching is always to be an affirming process.
- *Care* personally for the individual – respond to the needs of the coachee, recognising that it is appropriate at any time to stop everything to pray, being open to the emotions that are unlocked, being ready to refer as needed.
- *Strategise* plans – trying to eliminate the roadblocks and maximise the options and resources available to the coachee.

---

[18] For more detail we would recommend going to the source, and in particular two books to note – Steve Ogne & Tim Roehl, *Transformissional Coaching*, B&H Publishing, 2008; and Steven L. Ogne & Thomas P. Nebel, Empowering Leaders Through Coaching, Churchsmart Resources, 1996.

G.R.O.W.

- *Train* skills – training can be done in bursts, so long as the coach is careful not to fall into the all too easy trap of 'telling them what to do'. The trick here is to teach single skills, rather than going too broad.
- *Disciple* the whole person – not just the task. Leadership inevitably builds character and this needs to be recognised. This may involve the coach being called upon to offer support and accountability on issues that are drawn out.
- *Challenge* specifically – help to focus their goals and set some next steps... be specific, asking 'what will you do before next time we meet?' and so on.

YOUR NOTES ON THE CHAPTER...

7

PRACTICALITIES OF COACHING

So far we have explored many of the principles, skills and patterns of coaching. In this chapter we want to go a little deeper into the practicalities involved in the coaching relationship. This will include how to get a coaching relationship started, a whole range of typical elements of a coaching session and a variety of contexts in which your coaching can happen. To begin with, though, let's look at one practical process that has been developed by the international coaching-focused organisation Coachnet.

THE COACHNET PROCESS

Coachnet was started by Bob Logan in the 1990's and over the years has developed its own process that coaches can work through as they relate to both missional leaders and churches/mission teams.[19] It is represented as a cycle as shown in the diagram on page 108. It works perfectly with the GROW

---

[19] In addition to coaching individuals and small teams, Coachnet have also applied their experience to whole churches and have been central to the *Natural Church Development* insights that have emerged over the past 15 years. .For further information on Coachnet, including how to work with them, see their website - www.coachnet.org

progression and is based around five R's, which break down as follows:

Relate: Establishing the coaching relationship and agreeing the agenda for that relationship. This is the central axis of the whole process around which the rest of the R's work. It is also the first foundation to begin the coaching process. This important time includes exploring the hopes and intentions of the relationship, as well as agreeing the roles and establishing the boundaries. This can often be formalised in a simple 'coaching contract'.

There's no substitute for spending time building trust through getting to know one another and the first steps of accountability. This being the central axis, it is not so much a stage you move through as an ongoing developing feature that is connected to all the other four stages. Every session needs a relational element to reconnect near the beginning and will include agreeing the specifics of today's agenda and timetable.

As the coaching process develops, the relationship also grows and becomes an increasingly fruitful element of each of the remaining four R's.

Reflect: This process revolves around the strength of the relationship, but is given momentum by the identifying of key areas that need particular attention. These may come in the form of long-term ongoing issues or ones that have arisen since last meeting. They may involve areas of skill/gifting, or could be related to immediate events arising around instances that challenge, encourage, inspire or hurt.

This stage is about discovering and exploring those

issues – reflecting on them together to dig deep into where they have come from, any resulting impact they lead to, why they have had the impact they have and what are the potential future dangers (or conversely opportunities) that might come from them.

Refocus: Next comes a time of refocusing – looking away from the issues identified and towards Jesus, in order to turn away from what hinders or blinds us from God's perspective. This involves a blend of prayerful analysis and strategic decision making. As this happens, what the coach and missional leader are looking for is to discern what are the priorities to address more closely, and what are the next steps of action to take. It is precisely here in these two stages of **reflection** and **refocus** that the GROW steps will expand and sharpen the process.

Resource: As the missional leader has reached settled plans and made decisions for action from the reflections and refocusing, the coach continues to walk alongside them, not to feed a stream of ongoing information, but to provide necessary support and encouragement.

Review: Having been immersed in the detail, the time comes to step back and review the big picture. The missional leader can feedback their evaluation of the session and how they feel they have grown, been enlightened or challenged. The coach will have their own perspective from having watched the missional leader's engagement and reactions.

It's a time not only of evaluation but for celebration of the good things in the session and to make any final adjustment to the plans. It may very well conclude with thanksgiving for the journey together and prayer for the next stage. It's all keeping the momentum of the coaching 'wheel' on the move.

The Coachnet Coaching 'Wheel'

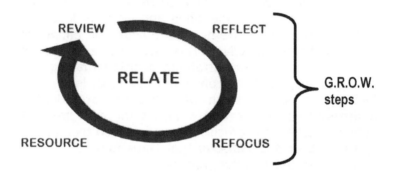

AGREEING ON THE COACHING PROCESS – A CONTRACT?

Once you have reached a common mind on the format for the coaching process, be that the Coachnet 'Wheel', another framework or even a less prescriptive process, it may be important that this and other practical details are formalised so that both parties are clear and you are building on an agreed foundation. Some will draw up a 'coaching contract' whilst others may just exchange some *Heads of Agreement*. Having something in writing is certainly helpful to go back to. Coachnet favour a contract and can provide outlines for reference.

Other coaching relationships arise as part of a training process for pioneers and teams, and continue after the training course ends. Certainly this is the case for the *mission shaped ministry* course produced by Fresh Expressions. The aim is for leaders to be linked with coach/mentors and the regional centre may well have a standard process and framework for these coaching relationships.

TYPICAL ELEMENTS OF A COACHING SESSION

Whatever the chosen format for coaching sessions, there are likely to be the same elements present. They won't necessarily all happen in every session, but will all be covered regularly in one way or another. We have highlighted twelve elements that we feel are essential to be central to the coaching process:

1. Each session should begin by agreeing a time frame and the agenda/objectives for the session, which needs to include the agreed priorities for that session. Doing this at the start will give the best chance of keeping on track and being able to work at a pace that isn't trying to cram in too much.

2. Sessions should start general, focusing on life issues and giving space to 'connect' at the relational level.

3. It may then be helpful in every session to review any recent developments, sharing in the encouragements and disappointments, and identifying the challenges or hopes.

4. Running in line with this, celebrating successes and blessings should be done whenever possible, keeping the context of the coaching relationship centred on where it can be discerned that God is at work.

5. Check progress on all aspects of previously agreed action. As we have already mentioned, this level of accountability is a crucial part of the coaching process. It will both highlight relevant areas for learning and help increased consistency of follow-through.

6. Explore application of mission and church planting principles from any recent training the leader has attended - the latest session of *mission shaped ministry*, for example. This works best when the coach is not only familiar with the key principles, but also with the particular syllabus of the course concerned. Reflecting on application of recent learning will be most effective to develop the leader and the project. We will highlight some specific missional church principles in the next chapter.

7. Spend time questioning and exploring in greater depth the ongoing issues/agenda areas that were agreed at the start of the session.

8. Take the opportunity to query things the missional leader is learning and things God is saying. This both keeps the missional leader accountable for their own personal walk with Jesus, but also encourages them to be thinking regularly about what God is saying through their prayer, the Word and their circumstances.

9. Summarise periodically to keep things on track and give feedback. This might be a feature of every session, but could even feature more than once in a session. This can assist keeping a record of key issues and Kairos events that require revisiting.

10. Encourage risk taking. It is in the nature of mission and missional leadership to push the

boundaries and pioneer in new ways. So risk is intrinsic to the enterprise and the coach needs to help openness to risk when walking in faith. Affirmation works hand in hand with this. As the pioneer is affirmed, their confidence is built up and their discernment of appropriate risk honed. Even when a risk taken doesn't prove fruitful, it is usually helpful to affirm the courage of the leader. This can release them from feeling the pressure to only ever make reliable decisions – which usually leads to no risks ever being taken and potential opportunities missed.

11.   Take notes and agree on new specific action. The action should have some form of time frame attached, whether to be reviewed at the next session or at a later date, and could include things such as study or time seeking the Lord.

12.   Make regular time for specific prayer and listening to God. In addition to particular times given to prayer, it is also important to try and remain open to the Holy Spirit throughout the session. Obviously, the more this is a central part of the process at all stages, the easier it is to hold close to God's will and keep Jesus at the centre of the coaching relationship.

DIFFERENT SETTINGS/CONTEXTS FOR COACHING

A very practical area to think through relates to the many possible contexts and settings for coaching sessions. There are a range of options, and there is no need to stick with just one, but it may help to have an idea of the breadth of session types as you make any plans in particular contexts, such as long-distance or with people you don't know so well. Here are a few of the ways we have seen coaching work:

1. The classic coaching session/meeting

This is most likely to take place in the home of either the coach or the missional leader or in their office. However, it might also take place in a neutral venue that is relaxed and 'safe', such as a meeting room or lounge, a café or restaurant. We particularly point these ideas out, because for some having snacks or meals through the session can help set a warm tone and relaxed atmosphere, whereas for others they may be a distraction.

Time of day is important in so far as it should be the most appropriate time possible for the missional leader. Often this is evening, but don't assume that morning or afternoon wouldn't be better. If the meeting is in the home then consider factors such as the possible distraction of other family members. And you may want to think about the comfort of lounge chairs (will they be relaxed... or encourage dozing?!), compared to the business-like gathering around the dining room table. We gather that for church planters in Russia, some specialize in kitchen table coaching!

2. Coaches visit to the mission context

In addition to the more regular sessions/meetings, as described above, it is important for coaches to visit missional leaders in their context. In addition to getting the feel of the area or social context, the coach should aim to experience one of the gatherings of the team and of the emerging fresh expression/mission initiative. This is important because it gives the coach a much better idea of the actual situation when they are processing things at a distance. It also provides first hand material for asking key questions and for seeing and sharing encouragements.

3. Retreats with review

Times away from both the missional leader's context and the regular place of coaching, be that home or wherever, can also be extremely valuable. Going away for a retreat to review progress can open up opportunities for deeper levels of honesty. A change of place, combined with the more relaxed time-scale, can give the impression of a new coaching context and so makes it easier to take a different approach or explore issues with new degrees of challenge.

The increased amount of shared time can also make a big difference in terms of building the strength and intimacy of relationship between the coach and leader, as well as more space to explore issues. Many also find the change of setting can renew a heart for listening closely to God and for hearing new insights.

4. Telephone coaching sessions

These are especially effective where distance is great. They ease pressure from both the coach and the missional leader, particularly in terms of covering enough ground in one session which has no room for extension due to travel time needing to be considered. They save cost as well as travel, and also open up the channels of communication between sessions. Even if you are coaching a missional leader locally, it can still be valuable to build in times of telephone communication, as it does give leaders the security of knowing that issues arising between sessions don't necessarily have to wait.

5. E-mail and correspondence

Similar to telephone coaching sessions, communication by email opens up the opportunity for issues to be shared between sessions and for the sense of ongoing journey to be developed further. It may not be the preferred mode of coaching in general, as it lacks the personal interface which can in turn leave big gaps for key personal issues to be ignored, and any form of conversation where tone of voice cannot be heard has the potential to be misunderstood. That being said, it is another available channel that can complement and be an excellent way of keeping the coach informed of developments as and when they happen, as well as being an excellent tool for accountability – regular reports written, encouragements and prayer requests shared, and so on.

In describing all these coaching settings we have assumed that we are relating to just one individual missional leader on their own. Whilst this may be most common, it may also be appropriate to coach a small team taking on a mission project or planting a fresh expression. We have also successfully coached leaders from two or three projects together. All the considerations of the possible different settings reviewed above still apply with more than one coachee. However, there are also a whole range of important new considerations that come into play and we explore these separately in the next chapter.

YOUR NOTES ON THE CHAPTER...

8

COACHING PIONEERS TOGETHER

Although it may be most usual to coach a single missional leader and focus exclusively on them, relating only to their single ministry situation or fresh expression, this is not always the case. Obviously as we open up the coaching process to more than one person and more than one project, all sorts of new complexities are introduced to both the relationship and the tasks involved. There are also limitations.

But be encouraged, almost all the skills and principles explored so far still apply – it's just that a whole new range of issues also need to be understood and managed. So we need to examine carefully these new challenges and changes presented. Now there is a progression of three possibilities that open up as we increase the components involved.

First, there is coaching a leadership or fresh expression team. This just adds people but sticks with a single context and project. Second, there is group coaching of more than one project, ideally with just one leader from each, but we have done it with more. Here we have diversity of relationships as well as projects and contexts. Finally, this can shift into more of a learning network and the coach may become more of a facilitator. Let's briefly look at the issues surrounding each of these three.

COACHING A MISSION TEAM

When coaching an individual leader we have recommended that an occasional visit to his/her team could be a really helpful addition as team is such an important factor in the leader's relationships and mission resources. However, sometimes a leader will want most or all of the coaching to be done with their team. This may be when the pioneer has adopted a particularly collaborative style of leadership with a leader team of two or three. Certainly plural leadership and teams are common in planting fresh expressions and it may be counter-productive to coach just one when the main dynamic of developing vision, values and strategy is in that team.

We shall now consider some of the specifics of coaching a team:

Practicalities

There are a few fairly obvious new practical things to take into account. Although some are details they can sometimes prove critical. Take managing the venue, for example. Making sure the venue is of a size and with the facilities to accommodate everyone suitably is essential. As the coach, it may be important where you sit so that you have good eye contact with everyone. In some venues/layouts there are seats to be avoided as they put you at a disadvantage. If there is a lead person in the team, it is best to be opposite them, not next to them where eye contact is least. And if you ever do co-coaching (both of us usually coach with our respective wives as we work well together), with a team in a circle, we've found it's better for us to be together rather than apart so that we are in close touch and others don't have to look from side to side.

Another practical factor is the size of the team. If it's more than three or four, it may get hard to maintain focus and effectively process options into decisions and plans. It can fall foul of the 'committee syndrome'. And so you may have to allow a little longer for a coaching session with more people involved.

A final practicality can be a real limitation, and that's fixing diary dates for meetings. Simply the more diaries to co-ordinate, the harder to find mutually convenient slots... unless the coaching session replaces the team's regular meeting date.

Process

Clearly many of the aims and functions of the coaching process just take on a corporate, multi-directional dimension. So the vital role of building a coaching relationship of familiarity and trust is now extended and can be complicated by different personalities involved. The coach must be sensitive to quieter, introvert team members and invest more into relationships that are slower to gel. Conversely it will be important not to let any character dominate too much.

While skills of listening are just as important, more management and conscious planning of who shares what is needed, so that a clear picture emerges at each stage. In the same way, for your 'good questions' to have their full effect you will need to weigh who to address them to. Do you address them always to the same team member, direct them in rotation or just generally to 'everyone' and allow random answers? This may be particularly important with follow-on questions. The need to think of these things can make the coach less relaxed and natural to begin with. If there is a clear team leader this may simplify some of these issues. If there is not, with the dynamics of communication in some teams, you may want to enlist the support of a 'chair person' to manage the process with you.

The management of the agenda also becomes a greater challenge as more people increases the interactions and also the potential diversions! In particular, the more structured parts of the coaching process like the GROW framework and SWOT analysis can be hard to keep on track. So it is important to make it more explicit and gain co-operation from the team.

Pay-offs

Don't forget that as well as extra challenges to coaching a team, there are some significant benefits. There is obviously the potential broad ownership as the whole team are involved in working to the decisions. And linked to this, it avoids the necessity for a second step of the leader 'selling' the plans to the team post coaching session. Obviously there are also more minds to bring to bear on each stage of the coaching process provided this is managed constructively.

Lastly, the coach will not only sense their growing relationship with the team but will also become aware of different team members' particular contributions. This can be a real enrichment if handled creatively. One member may be where encouragement is often to be found, another may foresee the problems, others may generate ideas, one may bring spiritual revelation and where are those averse to risk? All this adds to the fruitfulness of team coaching. And whereas when you coach an individual you devote whole sections to addressing questions and plans about the absent team, now it's happening right in the session.

GROUP COACHING MULTIPLE PROJECTS

As well as coaching individuals and teams, increasingly we have had experience of coaching leaders of more than one mission situation. We were first led to this when leading a one-year church planting course, which included three particular projects from Sheffield, Lincoln and Methyr Tidfill in Wales. There were monthly evening training sessions through a whole year with leaders and teams taking part. The leaders stayed overnight after each training evening and then we followed Morning Prayer and worship with group coaching through and over lunch the next day.

The benefits of contrasting three very different mission contexts and planting projects could have been outweighed by the complexities introduced. However, this was made manageable by the fact that we reviewed each project in relation to the planting principles that had been taught the evening before. This brought enough of the cohesion and congruence that proved for us to be the key.

As we have already seen with coaching teams, there are new dynamics just from increasing the numbers and consequently the interactions. And much that we have said about the joys and challenges of coaching teams also applies to groups only more so, with both multiple people *and* projects. And so the limitations are greater and have to be assessed carefully before everyone invests the time. They also need to be monitored regularly throughout the coaching journey.

Now from this introduction we can already see that there are contrasting pros and cons of this multi-dimensional group coaching as well as some limitations. So let's address these so that you can be clear of what you are taking on if you undertake this very demanding but potentially amazingly rewarding pattern of coaching.

Advantages

If there are a number of different projects represented in coaching sessions, and therefore a collected wealth of different experiences and wisdom, then there is great potential for cross-fertilisation within the group. As one missional leader shares their situation, the pool of potential ideas and helpful relevant experience is wider than it would otherwise be if limited to the interaction between leader and coach alone.

This strength of group coaching has produced some of the most rewarding ministry we have ever been involved in. The 'co-incidence' of relevant insight or a solution having cropped up from another, completely different, situation at just the right time has continually amazed us and we treasure several 'Ah ha!' moments from group coaching.

This not only relieves pressure from the coach, but can also help build a constructive atmosphere where missional leaders are not only being coached but also feeding into the lives and ministry of others as well as engaging in a shared journey between leaders in similar circumstances. This is creative synergy when it works well and a sort of 'peer coaching' emerges as the group relationships gel.

In addition to this, having more than one pioneer leader coached together can also be ideal to overcome any sense of isolation that people may be going through. So often missional leaders feel out on a limb, whether because they are the only pioneers in their church or part of the institution and are misunderstood by the rest of the congregation, or because they feel as though their sense of vision and call is at odds with what they have previously been taught church should be about.

It can be a real encouragement to meet regularly with other likeminded leaders who share a common sense of call and to realise they are not only not alone, but that their experience is normal and valuable. Like the previous advantage this can't be over-estimated. One can almost hear an audible sigh as leaders on the edge pioneering an untried path, discover one another and learn together.

Furthermore, group coaching provides a forum where there are more people praying for each initiative, more listeners with attentive ears to hear God's revelation and more gifts available to be able to discern ways forward and offer help. And this is taken to an extra level in group coaching compared to team coaching because leaders of other projects are more detached and able to listen objectively with more space to hear from God for the other project.

As the group coach themselves increase in awareness of these extra dimensions, they can naturally become open to the potential for spotting those missional leaders who themselves have coaching gifts and could be mentored into this role in time.

Finally, and certainly not to be disregarded, is the very practical advantage that it can help maximise the effectiveness of the coach's time. Several leaders and projects are coached in a single session and the increased pool of ideas, wisdom, experience and prayer also brings with it the potential for God to challenge and affirm several leaders at once with the same ongoing issues.

These are all considerable advantages, and as such group coaching is probably increasing for missional pioneers where the benefits may tend to work more than in other fields. However, do not enter into a group coaching situation lightly and before you have considered the potential disadvantages and limitations, and weighed up whether the situation is right to do so. Individual coaching can still often be the best course of action.

Disadvantages

The first disadvantage to point out is the obvious reduced exclusive focus on a single missional leader/initiative. Although we have seen the converse strengths, depending on the mix of people involved, there is definitely a dilution of attention on each project in one session. More people in the coaching relationship means less dedicated time, less individual prayer focus, and makes it harder to keep a regular accountable check of progress. More rigorous note taking is definitely needed to revisit agreed plans.

A second potential danger is that with more leaders comes more projects, and the tendency can be to let the project dimension dominate and get in the way of developing the leader and building the coach/missional leader relationship. This can happen very easily since it is the discovery of others with a common call that draws pioneers together in the first place.

However, as helpful as the shared task and journey can be, it can offer a convenient shield to hide behind where leaders don't have to share their personal struggles, and can draw attention away from how related the person and the project really are. Group coaches have to work to counteract these trends and keep an equal focus on growing the character and skills of each leader. It may also be that input from one leader to another may sometimes prove inappropriate and the coach needs sensitivity to correct this.

There is also more chance for diversions that take the coach off track, and it can be hard to manage against this happening. Of real significance is the fact that it is much harder to confront serious issues with others present and could therefore drain valuable time as the coach has to find times to meet with the leaders individually in addition to group meetings.

In this regard, the most threatening thing that we have experienced to the effectiveness of a coached group is when there is one leader among the others who doesn't seem to be able to respond well to the coaching process. As engagements with them and their project is confused it can spread confusion in a destructive way around the group. This highlights the extra importance of carefully selecting missional leaders really able to engage positively with the coaching process.

Also significant can be where one project is at a very different stage, so that even if the coach seeks to bring consistency of focus through tackling a selected area or principles, this may have limited success.

And lastly, as we have already indicated about a different issue, there is more pressure on time, meaning crucial aspects can be missed or one leader 'short-changed'. As such it is worth taking into consideration that longer sessions are generally recommended for group coaching.

Limitations

Linked to the inevitable increase in pressure of time with more leaders/projects, we would suggest that if your coaching sessions will usually be evening-based then two leaders is ideal, three may be just too many. We have tried it with three with some success – making careful note to give more time to a different project each session. But we would prefer having at least half a day if we are to do justice to coaching three missional projects together.

Another limitation already pointed to is that multiple focus coaching is bound to reduce the potential to delve really deep in each project every time. Also, there will often be less flexibility to take a leader at the point where they are in their situation and allow things to be shaped by what comes.

We have described group coaching where each project is represented by just one leader. This is a limitation that we would usually recommend. We have undertaken group coaching with three projects, one or two of which have had two from their team. However, this extra complication has meant that we only judged the success rate 50:50. In half the cases the extra complexities reduced the value to disappointing levels.

None of this need take away from the impact that group coaching can have. However, it is important to consider what the best context would be for the individuals concerned. Would they be likely to benefit from more focused one-on-one time, or would it be more helpful to have that sense of shared journey?

LEARNING NETWORKS & CO-COACHING

As we move from individual and team coaching to group coaching of several projects and leaders, we have observed that an added dimension progressively emerges of leaders beginning to coach one another. This points to another separate pattern of mutual support called *co-coaching* or *peer-coaching*, which involves people/leaders at a similar level of leadership or stage of life learning from one another[20].

Furthermore, in both group coaching and peer-coaching we are gaining more and more overlap with another related discipline known as *learning networks*. These take various forms but instead of a coach they rely on a facilitator whose role is less prominent than a coach and who exercises a lighter touch with the peer interactions becoming paramount.

---

[20] For further details on Christian peer-coaching and how it works, using processes that are very similar to the GROW model and based on asking SMART questions, we would recommend looking at the Coach22 website, which gives an overview as well as details of resources and training available to help you get peer-coaching up and running in your context. The web address is www.coach22.com and from there you need to click on 'peer-coaching' on the main menu.

As the life of a coached group of pioneers develops and their relationships grow in depth and confidence, and the coaching process bears its fruit, there is often a natural shifting of function to operate increasingly as a learning network. This can be no bad thing and it could be that it is agreed that there will be a conscious evolution into such a network.

The difference lies in the intention to learn from one another rather than having a coach to enable leaders to learn from their own experience.

Learning networks can function alongside a coaching relationship with individual missional leaders also being in the network, and they can complement each other very well. In fact one of the priorities that has emerged out of the Fresh Expressions movement in the last few years has been the need for shared learning and accountability between leaders of fresh expressions.

To enable this, learning networks are being promoted as one excellent forum for this to take place. In these networks people of similar heart and mission gather together to share their experience, best practice, collected wisdom and pray for one another. As we have described, this has overlap with many of the advantages of group coaching, particularly for promoting the sense of being a part of a wider movement of mission.

One particular type of learning network highlights similarities and differences with the coaching process. These are called Action Learning Networks[21]. These work to a clearly agreed pattern where members in turn

---

[21] For further details see www.actionlearningassociates.co.uk

will share an issue or challenge they are facing. Other members of the network are strictly limited to only asking questions in response until the member reaches their own conclusion or plan for action. This questioning is similar to parts of the coaching process and has the shared goal of developing the pioneer's own powers of analysis and problem solving – and owning their own solutions and decisions for action.

In contrast, other learning networks will start with this questioning focus but then add first the sharing of experience from within the group, then second the experience from sources outside the network, followed finally by waiting on God for his direct revelation. The reader should pick up the parallels with stages of the coaching process and the exploring of different quadrants of the Johari Window, explained in chapter three.

Another approach to Learning Networks that we have seen have a real impact is the 'Wildworks' model used by the European Church Planting Network (ECPN)[22] and others, which follows all the same phases as GROW-based coaching. The process itself, which has emerged from the business and industry world, is focused on creating 'Results-based conversations' as a format for shared learning and building skills. This is enabled through prioritising six key principles: *presence, discovery* and *work to win* (where the focus is *attitude*); and *knowledge, understanding* and *action* (where the focus is on *practical application*). They describe their process as open source learning communities

---

[22] For specific detail on the principles and values behind 'Wildworks' learning networks, see their website at www.wildworks.com. This has been set up not only to give details but mainly to make a whole range of resources available to help this process. The ECPN site can be found at www.ecpn.org.

We have been struck when we have experienced this model that it is worked out through four distinct phases. The first is for each member of the group to identify their purpose and the mission model they currently employ; the second, third and fourth then ask three questions i) What is; ii) What could be; iii) What will be.

Aside from the simplicity of this approach, and the very high effectiveness we have observed, we also note that these are essentially the same four stages as G.R.O.W., and so the same values are at the heart of Learning Networks as in coaching, with the intended goal the same of enabling both personal and ministry growth.

These particular ECPN/Wildworks learning networks function with a number of projects coming together, each represented by their leadership team. We have seen this work with up to a dozen teams with a maximum of four in each team. The process depends on expert facilitation and well developed routines and resources. But it delivers the very difficult as well as very rich combination of multiple projects and multiple teams all learning from and inspiring one another.

However, despite the similarities, it is important to recognize that learning networks, whatever the particular model they use, are essentially not coaching relationships. They are not reliant on the impartial ear and skilled guiding voice of external experienced coaches. We strongly recommend that missional leaders and pioneers of fresh expressions consider learning networks *alongside* individual coaching or following on from individual, team or group coaching.

For further information on the principles of learning networks, what happens and how they gather, see www.sharetheguide.org.

YOUR NOTES ON THE CHAPTER...

9

GETTING A RIGHT START WITH MISSIONAL PIONEERS

We have stressed that in any coaching it is important that key elements of the process and relationships are clear and agreed from the outset, and some sort of coaching contract may be appropriate. However, there are some specific issues with missional pioneers, church planters and those initiating fresh expressions of church that also need to be addressed.

In America, one of the favoured ways to begin the support and training of church planters is an initial 'boot camp' where planters are already linked to coaches who will then work alongside them for at least the first two years. These boot camps contain three foundational elements which we recommend can be built into the start of any coaching relationship with pioneers. It is so much better to have these things sorted out and clear, before moving on to the other details of the project which will always be impaired if these basics are shaky.

1. Clarifying and confirming the call

This can be done by meeting with the coach (and two or three others). Together they review the missional leader's past experience, and specifically look for evidence of pioneering motivation and fruitful initiating of new ventures in any previous roles and enterprise. They also seek to assess the leader's strengths and weaknesses.

Moving to the present ministry situation, together they hear how the leader has received their vision and sense of call to the new pioneering opportunity. A series of aptitude tests may be used to check for key qualities. Some examples of essential qualities and gifts to be looking for in missional leaders are that they are:

- Self motivated
- Catalytic in relationships
- Entrepreneurial/a pioneer
- A visionary, able to cast vision in a way that enables ownership
- A developer of people
- A good communicator
- Resilient and flexible
- Supported by their spouse (if they have one)

If the leader you are coaching is setting out on a pioneer project requiring real 'breakthrough' qualities and/or entrepreneurial flair, but is in fact not strong in these, no amount of good coaching or mentoring will produce real fruitfulness. However, we would qualify this by saying that in our experience the 'breakthrough' quality for a pioneering church plant or fresh expression can be delivered by two or three in a team where the overall leader may not on their own be so strong in this gifting. Prayer and discernment is needed as well as in-depth interview, analysis and some supporting exercises/questionnaires[23].

---

[23] For U.S. samples email admin@acpi.org.uk

2. Sharpening the vision

In these boot camps the missional leader takes a retreat at which their task is to expand their vision, committing it to paper under the following developed headings:

- Mission purpose
- Community values
- Priorities
- Initial people and plans

This written expanded vision is then the basis of a session with the coach to further sharpen it through a question and answer time. This ensures that right from the beginning of the coaching relationship the purpose and context is clear in the mind of both the coach and the leader. This is important so that matters can always be kept relevant and on track – using the original vision as a marker for when issues are not a priority, or to see how God is shaping the vision away from initial expectations.

3. Selecting and sifting the team

In this third and final foundational stage the missional leader meets with the coach to review those they are planning to call as leaders and core members of the mission team. Here the coach can challenge with questions about possibly unsuitable team members or dynamics, as well as possible omissions.

Even if the coaching relationship with your leader(s) does not include this sort of depth and thoroughness, we strongly recommend that you take time in an early session to review the following profiles of your leader(s) and their team:

Task, People, Principles: we all respond differently and have differing motivations towards these areas. There is a brief questionnaire which explores the priorities that team members give to areas of task, people and rules[24]. It is important where possible to have a balance between these strengths, and certainly not to have a team made up of all task-focused people (or the importance of relationship may get a little lost at the expense of getting the job done), or people-focused team members (who may focus too much on growing deeper relationships and on how others are impacted, leaving important tasks undone or not done well), or principles-focused people (who can get caught up in the rules to the extent of it being a barrier to tasks or relationships). A balance between these areas can draw in the strengths of each, and so form a very effective team.

Belbin team player strengths and weaknesses: here there is a longer questionnaire, which assesses the particular ways that individuals fit in and contribute to a team. This has come from research by Meredith Belbin[25], and highlights eight team roles that people contribute through their natural make-up - all of which are needed for a highly effective team. Each of us will be strong in two or three, which will reveal a lot about the type of people we are, how we like to work and how we work alongside others – drawing out both the advantages and the challenges to watch for.

Once the questionnaire has been completed there are resources to explain each team role and how they relate

---

[24] This can be downloaded from the ACPI website – www.acpi.org.uk or by emailing the ACPI office at admin@acpi.org.uk.

[25] Detailed explanation of the roles plus a questionnaire can be accessed at www.belbin.com

to one another. Again, this resource can help us to see how balanced the team is and through better awareness help individual members work best with one another and develop healthy team dynamics. This is invaluable for teams to recognise why they work well, or have struggles and so helps guide team members to recognising ways that they can change to work more to their strengths and draw less on their weaknesses.

The Belbin process can also enable leader and coach to identify any missing roles or those only weakly represented. If it's not possible to recruit new team to fill any gap, then special encouragement needs to be given to the existing team member who scores highest in this otherwise weaker team role.

We have observed in coaching pioneering enterprises that particular attention should be paid if you identify a missional team leader who happens to combine Belbin strengths in **Plant** plus **Monitor Evaluator** and also **Shaper**. This combination will mean that they are strong on generating original ideas and also good at evaluating which will and will not apply to the team situation. This will be experienced by the rest of the team as a real blessing in the early phase of a new project when the team lacks confidence and experience (the D1 and D2 phases explained in chapter one)

However, as the team matures and gains experience into the D3 phase, members look for participation in the ideas process. Also, if the leader's *Shaper* strength makes them push the tasks they have decided on, there can not only be a sense of lacking ownership, but also of control.

So leaders who happen to combine these strong roles, need the coach to be aware and provide special help and support to learn how to handle these strengths without negative outcome amongst the team over time.

Five-fold ministry role: again there are various tests available and one, that is in the form of a questionnaire, was put together by Mike Breen for the Pentagon of *LifeShapes*. It uses a series of experience-based questions, which together can help reveal which of the five-fold ministries from Ephesians 4:7-11 we most readily tend to express – be it apostlic, prophetic, evangelistic, pastoral or teaching.

Again, it helps us check that we have a fully rounded team with all orientations represented. But it also helps to recognise when God has drawn together a team that is weighted in particular ways, which can sometimes be a challenge to see new directions the Holy Spirit is leading in. For example, a team heavy in apostolic types may be imbalanced, or it may be called into a new phase of pioneering mission and quick multiplication. It is down to the processing between the coach and missional leader at this team-focused early stage to discern this.

Personality types: we have looked at a range of team member qualities, gifts and orientations that are important to understand in building an effective team to initiate mission and fresh expressions. Some will also want to look at insights and understanding that can be gained from recognising team member personalities. Classic among these are of course, the Myers Briggs type indicator (MBTI) assessments[26]. As we have emphasised for all aspects of coaching, here again increasing awareness enhances performance.

---

[26] See www.myersbriggs.org

4. Wider church relationships and gaining permissions

A final area specific to the early place of coaching pioneers in church mission and planting, is the need to recognise and respect relationships with other churches and to properly process and secure appropriate permissions. Here again it is important that those aspects are all thought through and clearly established in harmony before going further into the project. The issues of permissions will of course vary greatly according to the denomination and stream concerned. It is helpful if the coach is well briefed on these soon if from a different background themselves. Certainly all the relevant questions need to be asked and settled early in the coaching relationship[27].

In this short chapter we have highlighted certain key specific matters specific to missional church initiatives that the coach needs to review to lay a healthy foundation. As the project develops and the coach's supporting role develops there are many other aspects specific to mission, planting and fresh expressions that the coach needs to recognise and be familiar with. As well as generic coaching skills and processes covered in this book these are the particular issues relating to this mission field and whilst far too extensive to be covered in this book, a brief 'anatomy' of the areas is summarised in Appendix I.

---

[27] If you would like further assistance with any of these profiles referred to in this chapter, including resources or guidance on how to use them effectively, contact the ACPI team by emailing admin@acpi.org.uk

YOUR NOTES ON THE CHAPTER...

10

CONCLUDING REFLECTIONS

As we come to the end of this review of the principles and skills of coaching for mission pioneers and projects, we just want to take three last looks at the subject.

OUR TOP FIVE COACHING QUALITIES

Over and above all that we have explored we would highlight the following five qualities for coaches accompanying mission in the Kingdom of God:

1. An encourager with the 'Barnabas' gift

When the early church saw a breakthrough in mission to new contexts in Antioch, what did they do? They sent the one who was so marked out with the quality of encouragement that they had renamed him Barnabas – Son of Encouragement (Acts 4:36 and 11:19-22). He had the gift to see the evidence of the grace of God (11:23); know who was needed (11:25b) and how to maximise (11:24) and then multiply the work (13:1-3). Each of these qualities is central to the coaching role and provide invaluable spiritual enrichment to advancing God's kingdom.

2. Strong in the 'Helicopter' quality

Like a surgeon, the gifted missional coach can help to see both the big picture as well as the significant detail, whilst discerning the relationship between the two. This has sometimes been referred to as the 'helicopter' quality of rising up to see the broader horizon as well as dropping down to ground level. Such coaches are able to dissect a situation to uncover project 'anatomy' by the focused questioning that both pinpoints problems and releases answers relevant to the whole.

3. Function with 'incarnational instincts'.

Familiarity with mission endeavours and cultural awareness enable the coach to facilitate rigorously clear mission analysis. Their review and sharp probing should look for the fit between mission field, mission force and mission strategy (see Appendix I, page 149).

4. Faith that there is a way and patience to find it!

This is a tenacious faith to find where God is at work and to support and enhance a conviction that God has called and will enable. It works with patience to discover the way that God will release his promises (Hebrews 6:12). Whatever the presenting blocks or problems it has a driving conviction that somewhere in the situation and circumstances God will have a way.

5. Focusing action with accountability

Truly effective coaches know that identifying solutions and creative ideas has limited effect if not worked into a committed action plan with a clear accountability process. Decisions that lead to action must be followed by review of outcomes in turn leading to adjustment.

KEY SHIFT FROM TEACHER/TRAINER TO COACH

Many of us are used to the role of teacher as trainer but unfamiliar with coaching. Hence it is so important to remember that the coach is quite different from the teacher/trainer. Teacher/trainers take the missional leader/team through the principles in a planned, often linear, sequence. They can just have the one subject area in mind that today's course is focusing on.

By contrast the coach has to deal with whatever issues are raised today by the pioneer and planter and their context. These may come from widely differing subject areas. Hence, the coach has to have a much wider grasp of the whole range of principles, combined with the skill of being able to pull out from the complex matrix of principles, just the right one at the right time.

It's rather as though the teacher/trainer just has to hold one hand of thirteen cards and to play them in pre-planned sequence. Whereas the coach has to have the whole pack of fifty-two cards and to hold them in such a way that he/she can pull out any one in response to spontaneous situations as they arise.

In summary, the coach must know their mission and church plant stuff really well and be so familiar with it that they can spontaneously match the confronting challenge with the appropriate principles. This is why we have summarised in Appendix I some frameworks and arrangements of general missional principles to outline the ways that this can be facilitated.

KEEP ON LEARNING!

The nature of all principles of best practice is that they change and develop as your own experience and knowledge of others' stories grows. Consequently, we find ourselves in a constant state of perpetual learning and we can never know it all, but the more we explore and learn, the better prepared we will be as coaches to help other leaders to succeed in their vision and calling.

But this is no different from every area of Christian discipleship. Jesus calls us as followers and disciples and the root word for disciple is 'learner'. So disciples are lifelong learners and that's the key attitude for an effective coach who accompanies other disciples.

So we have now looked in depth at the principles and practice of coaching and mentoring leaders of church plants and fresh expressions. Our hope is that you have had enough input to have a clear idea of the challenge before you as you set out in coaching others, and that you feel inspired by the opportunity that you have been given to invest in other leaders and other mission initiatives and churches.

We would encourage you to continue using this book as a textbook that you can dip into or refer to as your coaching experience develops, and we hope that you can now build further connections to other coaches and leaders so that you might form a network of stories and experience that you can carry with you and build on through your continued journey with Christ.

APPENDICES

I.   Missional Church Principles at Your Fingertips

II. Project vs Person Scales

III. Core Character & Competencies of Coaches, Mentors, Accompanists and Spiritual Directors (work in progress)

IV. Going Deeper with G.R.O.W.

Bibliography

Appendix I

Missional Church Principles at Your Fingertips

So far, we have been exploring the general principles and skills involved in all coaching and referenced them wherever appropriate to their application to missional leaders and those pioneering fresh expressions of church. We have also looked at some specifics of helping pioneers lay healthy foundations in chapter nine. However, we now want to at least take a brief look at things the other way round and give pointers to some general issues of coaching that are more specific or even exclusive to working with pioneer missional leaders and those planting fresh expressions.

We mentioned in the Introduction and in point six of the essential elements of coaching sessions in chapter seven, that an understanding of current missional church principles is vital. Coaches need to be aware not only of what has emerged as the common lessons learned from previous mission experience, but also the important new lessons that are being learned. A good awareness of these principles will enable the coach to evaluate a missional leader's situation and equip them to probe and support pioneers to make creative decisions based on external experience.

Obviously there is a wide range of books and training manuals that describe a stream of wisdom and insight that can be applied, and many of these are very good and we would encourage you to draw on the books and experience of your own contacts that you feel are important. In chapter nine we also stressed the importance of being familiar with any missional training that your coachee is undertaking.

However, in this appendix we also include a brief description of some of the key principles that we have observed through ACPI and Fresh Expressions over the past twenty years. This is not the place to go into detail for each one, so this is only written to be a helpful guide for what you can explore further yourself.

In most instances we have produced, or will produce, resources that expand these principles more fully, and where this is the case we have mentioned them here and reference them more fully in Appendix IV.

In what follows we just offer a number of simple ways to frame and organise the many missional principles involved. Precisely because the field is complex and has to be available for random access by the coach, they need some sort of 'filing system'. And because it's complex the system or framework needs to be memorable as well as providing ready access so that principles can be 'pulled out' exactly as required.

If a coach has to have multiple complex principles at their fingertips to pull out whichever, whenever appropriate... then some ordering and frameworks are crucial. Bob Hopkins

3-DIMENSIONS OF CHURCH PLANTING PRINCIPLES

One way of thinking about missional church principles is that they come in three dimensions, which when put together form a fully rounded project. These dimensions, as with all 3D objects, are length, breadth and depth, and they unfold as follows:

Length – what sort of journey?

This is the **process** of mission engagement or church planting. There are many ways of describing these processes that have been developed, modelled and adapted over the years. It may not matter which process framework is used, so long as there is some strategic plan in place that can at the very least offer both an elementary checklist and a rough guide that can be veered to and from as the plant emerges. Planting a fresh expression of church that grows to maturity is a long journey with distinct phases and staging posts.

One well established analogy that provides a helpful framework for the principles involved is the *life cycle*, which is unpacked in the booklet *The Life Cycle of a Reproducing Church* (see Bibliography for details). However, others favour arranging the principles in different ways such as a tree, or multiplying yeast, etc. These frameworks are contrasted in an ACPI workbook (no.4 *Planning Frameworks*), which also seeks to integrate insight from both planning and 'discernment in context'. Coaches of fresh expressions really should be familiar with at least one or more of these frameworks.

Breadth – what sort of outcome?

This is the product of the process - the church plant, fresh expression or mission initiative itself. We can view it as the breadth because it is what makes the process visible, in the same way that length is not visible without breadth. As such, the outcome can change its form as vision, team and community come into being. Under this dimension you can gather issues such as the mission team and its evolving leadership. Key questions to be considering as the outcome unfolds are: what is church, when does the mission become church and what sort of church do you particularly want to grow?

Typical issues here will be: is the new missional community more a gathered church or church of the land; a bounded set or centred set; is it engaged with the context or distinct? And how does the community express itself in the small (cell), mid-size (congregation) and large (celebration)? We are rediscovering so much in the field of ecclesiology as mission-shaped thinking expands us 'out of the box'. Here ACPI has literature on cells and mid-size missional communities and a booklet planned on 'What is Church?'

Currently the Fresh Expressions *mission shaped ministry* course is one of the best ways to engage with these questions, and in addition ACPI can provide a UK and Australian workbook[28].

---

[28] The UK workbook is Bob Hopkins and Richard White, *Enabling Church Planting*, CPAS, 1995; the Australian workbook is Stuart P. Robinson, *Starting Mission-shaped Churches*, St Paul's Chatswood, 2007.

Depth – what sort of impact?

This can be a way of viewing the mission engagement of the fresh expression or church plant. Without mission engagement there is an absence of purpose in the outcome, a missing link to the process and a lack of Kingdom dimension. This mission engagement can be supported in many ways, which can include appreciating the importance of listening and mission audit, understanding and engaging with the culture, building connections with key people and organisations, as well as evangelism. To dig deep, breakthroughs are needed in evangelism but also in penetrating the post-modern culture with the kingdom of God in transformation. It will also be appropriate to look at how apostolic, prophetic and evangelistic roles can contribute to deliver engagement and impact.

ANOTHER WAY TO ARRANGE THE PRINCIPLES

A really fruitful way to approach the aspects of this discipline is to recognise three key components in any mission endeavour or planting. They are the **mission field** – everything to do with the context and culture; the **mission force** – everything to do with those called and committed to the engagement; and the **mission strategy** – everything to do with how the force engages with the field.

An extremely important overarching principle here is that there needs to be coherence between these three areas if mission effectiveness is to be strong and fruitful. We find some projects where there is significant mismatch between these three elements. And it is these three constituents that need to combine to produce the fourth element – the **mission outcome**, or fresh expression of church itself.

THREE CATEGORIES FOR THE MILITARY MINDED

For those who think in military or management terms, then again three headings may help them to organise the missional principles they require for ready access. Here the overall **purpose** and goal of mission will be the first, then key questions of **strategy and structure**, followed thirdly by key questions of **tactics and logistics**.

A SIMPLE LISTING OF THE PRINCIPLES

For other coaches, they may be able to work with a looser arrangement of mission and planting insights. This might arrange principles under these sort of headings:

- Vision and vision casting for ownership
- Listening and mission research
- Team, team building, personalities, roles and gifts
- Leadership and developing leaders
- Mission engagement and evangelism strategy
- Incorporating new believers and discipleship
- Gospel and culture
- What is church and fresh expressions of church
- Finances, charities and constitution

Again the curriculum of courses for pioneers such as *mission shaped ministry* provides this sort of categorisation, as do workbooks we have already referred to.

THE ACID TEST OF MISSION AND EVANGELISM

At one level, pioneering and planting fresh expressions of church stands or falls by the quality of engagement and evangelism. Clearly an understanding of mission and evangelism – how they differ, how they overlap and how to engage with each so as to release the optimum kingdom potential – is vital. They are often confused as being the same thing, but we would want to clarify that God's mission is the totality of his purposes to restore all of creation, whereas evangelism addresses restoration of humankind. Key issues to explore when thinking about this are:

Having an incarnational understanding

How can your church plant best reflect and serve the community you are reaching out to? This will not only determine what mission and evangelism happens, but also the whole pattern and style of church that develops as an indigenous expression through inculturation. In terms of approaches we think there are broadly three:

1. Attractional church – where you invite people to come to you;

2. Engaged church – where you go to the people, engage with them and their hopes and needs, but then invite them to come to you;

3. Emerging church – where you go to the people and stay with them, allowing whatever church expression to emerge from there.

More on this can be found in Bob Hopkins' article *Making Sense of Emerging Church* on the ACPI website.

Appropriate engagement

This might include developing an apt liturgy for your church plant that reflects the community you serve; or could be about developing an invitational sphere of contacts and ways to connect people to the Gospel. More on this can be found in Ann Morisy's chapter in *The Future of the Parish System*[29].

Building a strategic framework for evangelism

There are many excellent models and methods, but one we would point to that is easily learned and designed to be adaptable to your own context is the *LifeShapes Octagon*. This is written up in *The Passionate Church*[30], but a fuller exploration into this and a wider view of evangelism is written in the ACPI workbooks *Strategies of Evangelism 1* and *2*, available from the ACPI website.

Personal evangelism skills

Having built a strategic framework for evangelism, it is then important to hone the skills and develop the experience of your team in their evangelism skills, particularly in regard to prioritising the needs, hopes and aspirations of the specific people you relate to. Of the numerous helpful resources in this area, we would point again to the *Evangelism 1* and *2* workbooks, and also the excellent book *Sowing, Reaping, Keeping: People Sensitive Evangelism*[31].

---

[29] Ed. Steven Croft, Church House Publishing, 2006, chapter 9.

[30] *The Passionate Church*, written by Mike Breen and Walt Kallestad, published by Nexgen, 2004.

[31] *Sowing, Reaping, Keeping: People Sensitive Evangelism*, written by Laurence Singlehurst, published by Crossway, 1995.

CAUSES OF WEAK AND FAILED CHURCH PLANTS

One of the very best ways to learn about good practice of church planting and fresh expressions is to examine stories where weaknesses and failures have been prominent, and the reasons for them that have been identified.

Again, there are various resources available that explore lessons learned through both success and failure, and it may be that you know of particular examples through your own or others' experience that you can look to, and if this is the case we would certainly recommend it.

ACPI has produced a workbook, *Planters Problems*, which looks at some of the key reasons we have observed over the years, which include fixed mindsets, poor planning, issues of leadership, being inward focused, poor engagement and evangelism, cultural blindness, lack of team dynamics, team not being effectively released and being under resourced.

SUMMING UP

There will be more principles to consider, and you may already be able to think of other key aspects of church planting and starting fresh expressions that you need to address. But we hope that this appendix, though very brief, has given enough ideas to emphasise the importance of the coach developing their own systems to arrange the many principles of good practice.

Appendix II

Project vs Person Scales

These scales relate to the suggested review exercise described on page 17. We recommend that you return to this task regularly, but this page should be enough to get you through your first year as a coach. For each review mark both where you feel your focus is now, and where you want it to be.

At the start

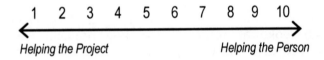

After 6 months

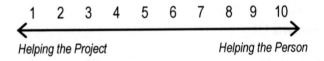

After 12 months

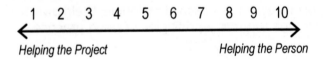

APPENDIX III

CORE CHARACTER & COMPETENCIES

There is currently a group representing Fresh Expressions, Church Army and Churches Together in Britain & Ireland that is reviewing the related roles of coaching, mentoring, accompaniment and spiritual direction with a view to identifying the core requirements of character and competency. What follows here is the work in progress document that they have so far developed:

This diagram was formed to illustrate the common character traits and competencies required for good practice in a range of Christian reflective practice. These include: accompaniment, coaching, consultancy, mentoring, spiritual direction, etc.

By **character** we mean that which is inherent in a person. Character is attitudinal and internally generated. Character is not unchangeable but grows over years rather than weeks. By **competency** we mean that skill or gift which can be learned or augmented by training.

Core Character:

Teachability
Humility
Listener
Empathetic
Emotional intelligence
Positive view of human potential and God's grace
Spirituality: - active, pervasive, integrated
Able and willing to take risks

Core Competencies:

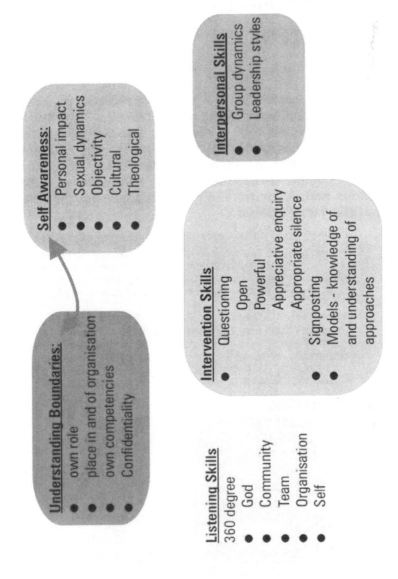

Self Awareness:
- Personal impact
- Sexual dynamics
- Objectivity
- Cultural
- Theological

Interpersonal Skills
- Group dynamics
- Leadership styles

Understanding Boundaries:
- own role
- place in and of organisation
- own competencies
- Confidentiality

Intervention Skills
- Questioning
  Open
  Powerful
  Appreciative enquiry
  Appropriate silence
- Signposting
- Models - knowledge of and understanding of approaches

Listening Skills
- 360 degree
- God
- Community
- Team
- Organisation
- Self

Tools and Training:

Self Awareness:
- Personal impact
- Sexual dynamics
- Objectivity
- Cultural
- Theological

Belbin, Disc, Mysers-Briggs, Enyeagram, etc

Understanding Boundaries:
- own role
- place in and of organisation
- own competencies
- Confidentiality

Interpersonal Skills
- Group dynamics
- Leadership styles

Listening Skills
360 degree
- God
- Community
- Team
- Organisation

Acorn Healing Trust

Intervention Skills
- Questioning
  - Open
  - Powerful
  - Appreciative enquiry
  - Appropriate silence
- Signposting
- Models - knowledge of and understanding of approaches

Appreciative Enquiry

Action Learning

General Tools and Training:

- CPAS – Arrow mentors
- Spiritual direction – cf Nick Helm, etc
- CRM – basic coaching and ICF coaching
- Training for Transformation – Partners (Dublin)
- ACPI – Coaching for Church Planters
- Mennonite conflict resolution
- Btec – Newcastle College (secular – life coaching)

MA Level:

- York St John – consultancy and mission
- Cliff College – Emerging Church and Accompaniment

APPENDIX IV

GOING DEEPER WITH GROW

There is plenty of material that is publicly available – especially on the web - which gives some practical examples of how the GROW process can be implemented.

The following two tables were shown to us by a colleague as helpful examples of GROW questions. In each case you will also note that they relate to the percentages of session time allocated to each stage that we mentioned at the end of chapter six (page 100).

Table 1: GROW Overview

		Content and possible questions	Contribution to the overall discussion
G	Goal	The goal, the direction, in which a coachee wishes to proceed may often be very uncertain. It is advisable to define goals that are attainable and at the same time attractive. *Possible question:* What do you want to achieve?	20%

R	Reality	Once we have a direction we further examine the reality of the coachee's situation. Here we want to gather objective information on where the person stands and what he/she has been doing so far. *Possible question:* What have you done that has worked for you so far? What obstacles slow you down?	
O	Options	At this stage we want to find as many alternatives as possible to find new ways forward or to solve the problem. It's about maximizing choices and generating new thinking. *Possible question:* What here are the opportunities for change?	60%
W	Will	Cross over into action. Define action steps, milestones and maybe a next date to talk about the implementation? Define the clear and specific steps to be taken: What's 1, 2 and 3? *Possible question:* What do you have to do next?	20%

Table 2: Sample G.R.O.W. Questions

Phases	Questions
Short description of problem/ concern	• How can I give you support? • What does the problem concern? • What is the topic of our meeting?
Goal (10%)	• What is your goal? • What do you ideally wish to achieve? • What would you like to have after our discussion? • What will assure you that you have achieved your goals? • What would it look or sound like? • Let's say your problem disappears overnight and tomorrow you find the situation changed for good. What will be changed and how? • What would be the elements of a good solution?
Reality (10%)	• Where do you stand now? • What have you done that has worked for you so far? • What is really the issue here, the bottom line? • Where would you position yourself on a scale of 0 to 10? (0 signifies a 'bad state', 10 signifies the 'perfect state'). What do you attribute to this rating? What works already? • Have you already been in a similar situation? If so, how did you solve the problem?
Options (60%)	• Where do you see opportunities for improvement? • What ideas come to your mind? • If you had all possibilities at your disposal, what would you do? • What are all the different ways in which you could approach this? • What would you have to do to move

	one step up the scale from 0 to 10? • What would you do if you could start again with a clean sheet? • What would your role model (e.g. mentor, best friend) advise in this situation? • What else could you do to improve the situation? What else?
Will (20%) **& close**	• What do you have to do first now? • What is the first/second/etc step on this path? • Which of the available possibilities is most attractive to you? • What will you specifically do? • How will you know that you've reached your goal? • Who will be able to help you reach your goal?

BIBLIOGRAPHY

John Whitmore, *Coaching for Performance: Growing People, Performance & Purpose*, (3rd Ed), Nicholas Brealy Publishing Ltd, 2002.

Robert E Logan & Sherilyn Carlton, *Coaching 101*, Churchsmart, 2003.

John Whitmore, Laura Whitworth, Henry Kimsey-House, Phil Sandahl, *Co-active Coaching: New Skills for Coaching People Toward Success in Work and Life*, Davies-Black Publishing, 1998.

Mission-shaped Church, Church House Publishing, 2004.

Mike Breen & Walt Kallestad, *The Passionate Church*, Nexgen, 2004.

Mike Breen & Walt Kallestad, *A Passionate Life*, Nexgen, 2004.

Bob & Mary Hopkins, *Strategies for Evangelism & Role of Evangelist workbooks 1 & 2*, ACPI, 2007.

Bob & Mary Hopkins, *Frameworks and Analogies*, ACPI, 2008.

Bob Hopkins, *Planters Problems*, ACPI, 2008.

Bob Hopkins, *Explaining Cell Church* (2nd Ed), ACPI, 2008

Bob Hopkins & Richard White, *Enabling Church Planting*, CPAS, 1995

Laurence Singlehurst, *Sowing Reaping Keeping: People Sensitive Evangelism*, Crossways, 1995.

Bob Hopkins & Mike Breen, *Clusters: Creative Mid-sized Missional Communities*, 3dm, 2007.

Bob Hopkins, *Cell Stories as Signs of Mission*, Grove Books, 2000.

Steve Croft, Freddy Hedley & Bob Hopkins, *Listening for Mission*, Church House Publishing, 2006.

Freddy Hedley, *Lessons from Antioch*, Emblem, 2007.

Joseph O'Connor & John Seymour, *Introducing NLP*, HarperCollins, 1990.

Steven Croft (ed), *The Future of the Parish System*, Church House Publishing, 2006.

Stuart P. Robinson, *Starting Mission-shaped Churches*, St Paul's Chatswood, 2007.

Tony Stoltzfus, *Leadership Coaching*, Coach22, 2005.

Bruce Patrick, *Life Cycle of a Reproducing Church* (2nd Ed), ACPI, 2006.

Lightning Source UK Ltd.
Milton Keynes UK
13 October 2010

161202UK00007B/48/P